Learning Science Through Computer Games and Simulations

Committee on Science Learning:
Computer Games, Simulations, and Education

Margaret A. Honey and Margaret L. Hilton, *Editors*

Board on Science Education

Division of Behavioral and Social Sciences and Education

NATIONAL RESEARCH COUNCIL
OF THE NATIONAL ACADEMIES

THE NATIONAL ACADEMIES PRESS
Washington, D.C.
www.nap.edu

THE NATIONAL ACADEMIES PRESS   500 Fifth Street, N.W.   Washington, DC 20001

NOTICE: The project that is the subject of this report was approved by the Governing Board of the National Research Council, whose members are drawn from the councils of the National Academy of Sciences, the National Academy of Engineering, and the Institute of Medicine. The members of the committee responsible for the report were chosen for their special competences and with regard for appropriate balance.

This study was supported by Contract No. DRL-0836206 between the National Academy of Sciences and the National Science Foundation and Contract No. 2008-2457 between the National Academy of Sciences and the William and Flora Hewlett Foundation. Any opinions, findings, conclusions, or recommendations expressed in this publication are those of the authors and do not necessarily reflect the views of the organizations or agencies that provided support for the project.

Library of Congress Cataloging-in-Publication Data

Learning science : computer games, simulations, and education / Committee on Science Learning ; Margaret A. Honey and Margaret Hilton, editors.
    p. cm.
    Includes bibliographical references and index.
    ISBN 978-0-309-18523-3 (hardcover : alk. paper) — ISBN 978-0-309-18524-0 (pdf : alk. paper) 1. Science—Study and teaching (Elementary) 2. Science—Study and teaching (Secondary) I. Honey, Margaret. II. Hilton, Margaret. III. National Research Council. Committee on Science Learning.
    LB1585.L357 2011
    372.35′044—dc22

                              2011004594

Additional copies of this report are available from the National Academies Press, 500 Fifth Street, N.W., Lockbox 285, Washington, DC 20055; (800) 624-6242 or (202) 334-3313 (in the Washington metropolitan area); Internet, http://www.nap.edu

Suggested citation: National Research Council. (2011). *Learning Science Through Computer Games and Simulations*. Committee on Science Learning: Computer Games, Simulations, and Education, Margaret A. Honey and Margaret L. Hilton, Eds. Board on Science Education, Division of Behavioral and Social Sciences and Education. Washington, DC: The National Academies Press.

THE NATIONAL ACADEMIES
Advisers to the Nation on Science, Engineering, and Medicine

The **National Academy of Sciences** is a private, nonprofit, self-perpetuating society of distinguished scholars engaged in scientific and engineering research, dedicated to the furtherance of science and technology and to their use for the general welfare. Upon the authority of the charter granted to it by the Congress in 1863, the Academy has a mandate that requires it to advise the federal government on scientific and technical matters. Dr. Ralph J. Cicerone is president of the National Academy of Sciences.

The **National Academy of Engineering** was established in 1964, under the charter of the National Academy of Sciences, as a parallel organization of outstanding engineers. It is autonomous in its administration and in the selection of its members, sharing with the National Academy of Sciences the responsibility for advising the federal government. The National Academy of Engineering also sponsors engineering programs aimed at meeting national needs, encourages education and research, and recognizes the superior achievements of engineers. Dr. Charles M. Vest is president of the National Academy of Engineering.

The **Institute of Medicine** was established in 1970 by the National Academy of Sciences to secure the services of eminent members of appropriate professions in the examination of policy matters pertaining to the health of the public. The Institute acts under the responsibility given to the National Academy of Sciences by its congressional charter to be an adviser to the federal government and, upon its own initiative, to identify issues of medical care, research, and education. Dr. Harvey V. Fineberg is president of the Institute of Medicine.

The **National Research Council** was organized by the National Academy of Sciences in 1916 to associate the broad community of science and technology with the Academy's purposes of furthering knowledge and advising the federal government. Functioning in accordance with general policies determined by the Academy, the Council has become the principal operating agency of both the National Academy of Sciences and the National Academy of Engineering in providing services to the government, the public, and the scientific and engineering communities. The Council is administered jointly by both Academies and the Institute of Medicine. Dr. Ralph J. Cicerone and Dr. Charles M. Vest are chair and vice chair, respectively, of the National Research Council.

www.national-academies.org

COMMITTEE ON SCIENCE LEARNING: COMPUTER GAMES, SIMULATIONS, AND EDUCATION

MARGARET A. HONEY (*Chair*), New York Hall of Science, Queens
WILLIAM B. BONVILLIAN, Washington, DC, Office, Massachusetts Institute of Technology
JANIS CANNON-BOWERS, Institute for Simulation and Training, University of Central Florida
ERIC KLOPFER, Department of Urban Studies and Planning, Massachusetts Institute of Technology
JAMES W. PELLEGRINO, Learning Sciences Research Institute, University of Illinois, Chicago
RAY PEREZ, Office of Naval Research, Arlington, Virginia
NICHOLE PINKARD, College of Computing and Digital Media, DePaul University
DANIEL SCHWARTZ, School of Education, Stanford University
CONSTANCE STEINKUEHLER, School of Education, University of Wisconsin, Madison
CARL E. WIEMAN, Carl Wieman Science Education Initiative, University of British Columbia (until March 2010)

MARTIN STORKSDIECK, *Study Director* (since June 2010)
J. REID SCHWEBACH, *Study Director* (until May 2010)
MARGARET L. HILTON, *Senior Program Officer*
REBECCA KRONE, *Program Associate*
PATRICIA HARVEY, *Senior Program Assistant* (until July 2009)
WUNIKA MUKAN, *Program Assistant* (until December 2009)

Acknowledgments

The committee and staff thank the many individuals and organizations who assisted us in our work and without whom this study could not have been completed. First, we acknowledge the generous support of the National Science Foundation (NSF) and the William and Flora Hewlett Foundation. We are particularly grateful to Marshall (Mike) S. Smith, former program director for education at the William and Flora Hewlett Foundation, who identified the need for such a study and made the initial request. We also thank John C. Cherniavsky, senior advisor for research in the NSF Division of Research on Learning in Formal and Informal Settings, for his support of the study.

Individually and collectively, committee members benefited from discussions that grew out of the papers and presentations from the October 2009 workshop. We are grateful to each of the presenters, many of whom also wrote papers on different aspects of simulations, games, and science learning. They include Eva Baker, University of California, Los Angeles; Sasha Barab, Indiana University; Daphne Bavelier, University of Rochester; John Behrens, Cisco Networking Academy; Alex Chisolm, Learning Games Network; Douglas Clark, Vanderbilt University; Katherine Culp, Education Development Center; Ton de Jong, University of Twente, The Netherlands; Christopher Dede, Harvard University; Daniel Edelson, National Geographic Society; Dexter Fletcher, Institute for Defense Analyses; Alan Gershenfeld, E-Line Ventures; Robert Goldstone, Indiana University; Richard Halverson, University of Wisconsin, Madison; John Hight, Sony Computer Entertainment of America; Paul Horwitz, The Concord Consortium; Mizuko Ito, University of California, Irvine; Yasmin B. Kafai, University of Pennsylvania; Diane J. Ketelhut, Temple University; Merrilea J. Mayo, Kauffman Foundation; Scot Osterweil, Massachusetts Institute of Technology; Jan L. Plass, New York University; Edys Quellmalz, WestEd; Steven Schneider, WestEd; Valerie J.

Shute, Florida State University; Nancy B. Songer, University of Michigan; Kurt D. Squire, University of Wisconsin, Madison; Reed Stevens, Northwestern University; Ronald H. Stevens, University of California, Los Angeles; Michael J. Timms, WestEd; Ellen A. Wartella, University of California, Riverside; and Susan Zelman, Corporation for Public Broadcasting.

Many individuals at the National Research Council (NRC) assisted the committee. Center for Education director Patricia Morison, Board on Science Education deputy director Heidi Schweingruber, and Board on Science Education director Martin Storksdieck offered valuable suggestions at our committee meetings, as well as providing helpful comments on drafts of the report. Reid Schwebach, study director until May 2010, worked closely with the committee to design and carry out the workshop, commission valuable papers and presentations, and write initial drafts of the report. Senior program officer Margaret Hilton assisted the committee with subsequent drafts.

We thank Kirsten Sampson Snyder, who shepherded the report through the NRC review process; Christine McShane, who edited the draft report; and Yvonne Wise for processing the report through final production. We are grateful to Patricia Harvey, who arranged logistics for the first committee meeting; Wunika Mukan for her able assistance in arranging the workshop and final two committee meetings; and Rebecca Krone for her assistance with editing and preparing the manuscript for review and final publication.

This report has been reviewed in draft form by individuals chosen for their diverse perspectives and technical expertise, in accordance with procedures approved by the NRC's Report Review Committee. The purpose of this independent review is to provide candid and critical comments that will assist the institution in making its published report as sound as possible and to ensure that the report meets institutional standards for objectivity, evidence, and responsiveness to the study charge. The review comments and draft manuscript remain confidential to protect the integrity of the deliberative process. We thank the following individuals for their review of this report: Christopher Dede, Learning Technologies, Harvard Graduate School of Education; Chad Dorsey, president, The Concord Consortium, Concord, MA; Pamela R. Jeffries, associate dean for academic affairs, Johns Hopkins University School of Nursing; Ken Koedinger, School of Computer Science, Carnegie Mellon University; Marcia C. Linn, Education in Mathematics, Science, and Technology, University of California, Berkeley; William L. McGill, Information Sciences and Technology, Pennsylvania State University; Catherine Milne, Department of Teaching and Learning, Steinhardt School of Culture, Education, and Human Development, New York University; Jan L. Plass, Educational Communication and Technology, Steinhardt School, New York University; Brooke M. Whiteford, Technology Assisted Learning Division, RTI International; Diego Zapata-Rivera, Research and Development, Educational

Testing Service; and Michael J. Zyda, GamePipe Laboratory, Department of Computer Science, University of Southern California.

Although the reviewers listed above provided many constructive comments and suggestions, they were not asked to endorse the content of the report nor did they see the final draft of the report before its release. Adam Gamoran, Wisconsin Center for Education Research, University of Wisconsin, Madison, and Stephen Fienberg, Department of Statistics, Carnegie Mellon University, oversaw the review of this report. Appointed by the NRC, they were responsible for making certain that an independent examination of this report was carried out in accordance with institutional procedures and that all review comments were carefully considered. Responsibility for the final content of this report rests entirely with the author and the institution.

Finally, we thank our colleagues on the committee for their enthusiasm, hard work, and collaborative spirit in writing this report.

Margaret A. Honey, *Chair*
Martin Storksdieck, *Study Director*
Committee on Science Learning:
Computer Games, Simulations, and Education

Contents

Executive Summary

At a time when scientific and technological competence is vital to the nation's future, the weak science achievement of U.S. students reflects the uneven quality of science education. Although children come to school with innate curiosity about the natural world, science classes rarely foster their interest. Students spend time listening to lectures, carrying out preordained "cookbook" laboratory activities, and memorizing the science facts that are emphasized in current high-stakes tests, losing interest in science as they move beyond elementary school. Many graduate from high school without the science knowledge that could be of enormous value in their future lives, as informed citizens or as members of the scientific and technical workforce.

Many experts call for a new approach to science education, based in cognitive research. In this approach, teachers spark students' interest by engaging them in investigations, helping them to develop understanding of both science concepts and science processes while maintaining motivation for science learning.

Computer simulations and games have great potential to catalyze this new approach. They enable learners to see and interact with representations of natural phenomena that would otherwise be impossible to observe—a process that helps them to formulate scientifically correct explanations for these phenomena. Simulations and games can motivate learners with challenges and rapid feedback and tailor instruction to individual learners' needs and interests. To explore this potential, the National Science Foundation and the William and Flora Hewlett Foundation charged the National Research Council:

> An ad hoc committee will plan and conduct a two-day workshop to explore the connections between what is known about science learning and computer gaming and simulations, the role computer gaming and simulations

1

could play in assessing learning, and the pathways by which they could be used on a large scale. Following the workshop, the committee will meet to discuss the existing evidence, drawing on the presentations and materials shared at the workshop, and come to consensus about priorities for a future research agenda. It will write a report that summarizes the workshop and provides the committee's conclusions and recommendations about a future research agenda in this area.

The workshop agenda will address the three critical topics highlighted above and provide the basis for the development of a research agenda. The workshop will feature invited presentations and discussions of available research evidence and discuss possible research pathways for obtaining answers to three core questions:

1. What is the connection between learning theory and computer gaming and simulations?
2. What role could computer gaming and simulations play in the assessment of student learning?
3. What are the pathways by which computer gaming and simulation could materialize at sufficient scale to fully evaluate their learning and assessment potential?

Although research on how simulations and games support science learning has not kept pace with the rapid development of these new learning technologies, the evidence was sufficient to reach the conclusions summarized here.

Simulations and games are both based on computer models and allow user interactions, but each has unique features. Simulations are dynamic computer models that allow users to explore the implications of manipulating or modifying parameters within them. Games are often played in informal contexts for fun, incorporate explicit goals and rules, and provide feedback on the player's progress. In a game, the player's actions affect the state of play.

The committee views simulations and games as worthy of future investment and investigation as a means to improve science learning. Simulations and games have potential to advance multiple science learning goals, including motivation to learn science, conceptual understanding, science process skills, understanding of the nature of science, scientific discourse and argumentation, and identification with science and science learning.

Most studies of simulations have focused on conceptual understanding, providing promising evidence that simulations can advance this science learning goal. There is moderate evidence that simulations motivate students' interest in science and science learning, and less evidence about whether they support other science learning goals.

Evidence for the effectiveness of games for supporting science learning is emerging but is currently inconclusive. To date, the research base is very limited.

Gaps and weaknesses in the research on simulations and games make it difficult to build a coherent base of evidence that could demonstrate their effectiveness and inform improvements. The proposed research agenda takes a stronger, more systematic approach to research and development.

To strengthen the overall quality of the research:

- Researchers and developers should clearly specify the desired learning outcomes of a simulation or game and describe in detail how it is expected to advance these outcomes. They should describe the design features that are hypothesized to activate learning, the intended use of these design features, and the underlying learning theory. This will allow research findings to accumulate, providing a base for improved designs and enhanced effectiveness for learning.
- Researchers should initially develop methodologies for both design and evaluation that focus on continual improvement. The use of such methodologies will help to ensure that large studies are not outdated by the time they are published due to rapid changes in technology and advances in cognitive science.

The committee's full research agenda (in Chapter 7) recommends targeted research to increase understanding of the following topics:

- the role of simulations and games in learning,
- using them in formal and informal contexts,
- using them to assess and support individualized learning, and
- scaling up simulations and games.

To facilitate ongoing improvement in simulations and games for science learning:

- Academic researchers, developers and entrepreneurs from the gaming industry, and education practitioners and policy makers should form research and development partnerships to facilitate rich intellectual collaboration. These partnerships, which may be large or small, should coordinate and share information internally and with other partnerships.
- Government agencies and foundations may consider the potential benefits of providing sustained support for such partnerships.

This research agenda is intended to provide guidance to active and prospective researchers, simulation and game developers, commercial publishers, and funders. In the future, the agenda will have to adapt and evolve along with the continued rapid evolution of educational simulations and games.

1

Introduction

This chapter opens with a description of the uneven quality of students' science achievement and of current science education in America. The second section describes the committee's charge to explore the potential of computer simulations and gaming to improve science learning, its approach, and the organization of this report. In the third section, the committee defines simulations and games, with examples. The fourth section highlights the potential of simulation and games to support science learning, and the gaps in the research on this potential. The chapter ends with conclusions.

SCIENCE EDUCATION CHALLENGES

The science achievement of U.S. elementary and secondary students is uneven. The "nation's report card" from the National Assessment of Educational Progress, shows that student science scores were stagnant between 1996 and 2005, and disparities in the performance of students of different races and socioeconomic status persisted (Grigg, Lauko, and Brockway, 2006). On the 2006 science test of the Program for International Student Assessment (PISA), U.S. 15-year-olds scored below the average among 30 industrialized nations (Organisation for Economic Co-operation and Development, 2007).

These trends are worrisome for two reasons. First, some of today's science students will become the next generation of scientists, engineers, and technical workers, creating the innovations that fuel economic growth and international competitiveness (National Academy of Sciences, National Academy of Engineering, and Institute of Medicine, 2007; U.S. President, 2009). A lack of high-achieving science students today could constrain the future scientific and technical workforce. Second, today's science students will become tomorrow's citizens, who will require understanding of science

5

and technology to make informed decisions about critical social scientific issues, ranging from global warming to personal medical treatments. Adults in the United States have a naïve understanding of science concepts and the nature of science (National Research Council, 2007; Pew Research Center and American Association for the Advancement of Science, 2009), and the uneven science achievement of current K-12 students threatens to perpetuate this problem.

U.S. students' limited science knowledge results partly from a lack of interest in science and motivation to persist in mastering difficult science concepts, and this lack of interest in, in turn, is related to current approaches to science education (National Research Council, 2005b, 2007). Although young children come to school with innate curiosity and intuitive ideas about the world around them, science classes rarely tap this potential. In elementary and secondary science classrooms, students often spend time memorizing discrete science facts, rather than developing deep conceptual understanding. Partly because of a focus on improving student performance on high-stakes accountability tests, science classes typically provide students with few opportunities to conduct investigations, directly observe natural phenomena, or work to formulate scientific explanations for these phenomena (Banilower et al., 2008; National Research Council, 2005b).

Over time, students no longer see science as connected to the real world and lose interest in the subject, especially as they move from elementary to middle school (Cavallo and Laubach, 2001; Cohen-Scali, 2003; Gibson and Chase, 2002; Ma and Wilkins, 2002). Within this overall pattern, girls, minorities, students from single-parent homes, and students living in poor socioeconomic conditions generally have more negative perceptions of science than do boys, whites, students from two-parent families, and students with high socioeconomic status (Barman, 1999; Blosser, 1990; Ma and Ma, 2004; Ma and Wilkins, 2002). Among middle and high school students responding to a recent national survey, only half viewed science as important for success in high school and college, and only about 20 percent expressed interest in a science career (Project Tomorrow and PASCO Scientific, 2008).

COMMITTEE CHARGE AND APPROACH

To explore the potential of computer simulations and games to address these critical science education challenges, the National Science Foundation and the William and Flora Hewlett Foundation charged the National Research Council as follows (see Box 1-1).

To carry out the charge, the board convened the Committee on Science Learning: Computer Games, Simulations, and Education, with representation from science education and learning in science, pedagogy, the design of games and simulations, the design of online learning environments, the

---

BOX 1-1
Study Charge

An ad hoc committee will plan and conduct a two-day workshop to explore the connections between what is known about science learning and computer gaming and simulations, the role computer gaming and simulations could play in assessing learning, and the pathways by which they could be used on a large scale. Following the workshop, the committee will meet to discuss the existing evidence, drawing on the presentations and materials shared at the workshop, and come to consensus about priorities for a future research agenda. It will write a report that summarizes the workshop and provides the committee's conclusions and recommendations about a future research agenda in this area.

The workshop agenda will address the three critical topics highlighted above and provide the basis for the development of a research agenda. The workshop will feature invited presentations and discussions of available research evidence and discuss possible research pathways for obtaining answers to three core questions:

1. What is the connection between learning theory and computer gaming and simulations?
2. What role could computer gaming and simulations play in the assessment of student learning?
3. What are the pathways by which computer gaming and simulation could materialize at sufficient scale to fully evaluate their learning and assessment potential?

---

assessment and applications of technology to assessment, cognitive science, educational technology, and the use of gaming and simulations for training. The committee addressed the charge through an interactive process of deliberation, information gathering, and writing and revising this report.

Committee discussions and preliminary writing informed the design of a two-day workshop held in October 2009. In preparation for the workshop, the committee commissioned 11 papers to review the research related to the study charge (see Appendix A). To explore each topic from multiple perspectives, the committee asked a primary author (or authors) to synthesize the available research, a second author to draft a short response paper, and a panel of experts to further elaborate on the topic. The papers and responses were presented at the workshop; they are available online at http://www7. nationalacademies.org/bose/Gaming_Sims_Homepage.html.

Although the commissioned papers served as a primary information source for this report, the committee interpreted the papers in light of other information and its own expert judgment, selecting what portions to include. These deliberations inform the committee's conclusions and recommendations for future research. Because of limits on time and resources, this report focuses primarily on the use of games and simulations in K-12 science learning, with less attention to their use in higher education.

Organization of the Report

Following this introductory chapter, the next chapter examines the available evidence on the effectiveness of simulations and games for science learning. Chapter 3 considers the use of simulations and games in formal instructional contexts, including schools and undergraduate classrooms, and Chapter 4 examines what is known about them in informal contexts, such as homes, after-school programs, and science centers. Chapter 5 explores the growing use of games and simulations as tools for assessment of student science learning, and Chapter 6 considers issues related to bringing them into use on a wider scale. Each chapter ends with conclusions, and Chapter 7 presents the committee's recommended agenda to guide future research and development of games and simulations for science learning.

DEFINING SIMULATIONS AND GAMES

An important step in carrying out the committee charge was to establish shared definitions of computer simulations and games to provide a clear focus for the study.

Simulations and games lie along a continuum, sharing several important characteristics. Both are based on computer models that simulate natural, engineered, or invented phenomena. Most games are built on simulations, incorporating them as part of their basic architecture. Because of this close relationship, the recent rapid advances in computer hardware and software that have led to improvements in computer modeling and in the fidelity of simulations have enhanced games as well as simulations (National Research Council, 2010). Both simulations and games allow the user to interact with them, and they also provide at least some degree of user control. These similarities were noted by a separate National Academies committee, which recently observed, "The technical and cultural boundaries between modeling, simulation, and games are increasingly blurring" (National Research Council, 2010, p. 1).

Simulations and games also differ in several important respects, as discussed below.

Simulations

Simulations are computational models of real or hypothesized situations or natural phenomena that allow users to explore the implications of manipulating or modifying parameters within them (Clark et al., 2009). Plass, Homer, and Hayward (2009) propose that a simulation differs from a static visualization (e.g., a diagram in a textbook) because it is dynamic, and differs from a dynamic visualization (an animation) because it allows user interaction. Other experts, however, use the term "visualization" to refer to a simulation that allows interactivity. For example, Linn and colleagues (2010) define visualizations as "interactive, computer-based animations (such as models, simulations, and virtual experiments) of scientific phenomena." Reflecting this variation, this report will use the terms "simulation" and "interactive visualization" interchangeably.

Simulations allow users to observe and interact with representations of processes that would otherwise be invisible. These features make simulations valuable for understanding and predicting the behavior of a variety of phenomena, ranging from financial markets to population growth and food production. Scientists routinely develop and apply simulations to model and understand natural phenomena across a wide range of scales, from subatomic to planetary.

This report focuses on simulations that are designed specifically to support science learning among students of all ages.

Games

Computer games differ from simulations in several ways. Perhaps most importantly, games are played spontaneously in informal contexts for fun and enjoyment, whereas users typically interact with a simulation in a formal context, such as a science class or workplace. In addition, games generally incorporate explicit goals and rules. These two features of games are shared by both computer and traditional games, including board games such as *Chess* or *Monopoly* and outdoor games such as *Capture the Flag*. Computer games also differ from computer simulations in two other ways: (1) they provide feedback to measure the player's progress toward goals, and (2) the player's actions and overall game play strategies influence the state of the game—the overall digital "world" and the player's further interactions with it (Clark et al., 2009; Hays, 2005). Although many games include an element of competition, and this increases enjoyment for some individuals, not all games are competitive.

Commercial computer games, designed for entertainment, have grown increasingly popular over the past two decades. Gaming hardware and software have evolved, and individuals today access and play games from a variety of platforms, including video consoles, personal computers, and cell phones. Game play is increasingly incorporated within online social networking (Hight, 2009). Domestic sales of computer and video game software reached $11.7 billion in 2008 (Entertainment Software Association, 2010), comparable to domestic motion picture box office sales that year of $10 billion (Motion Picture Association of America, 2010). A recent national survey of young Americans aged 8 to 18 found that their use of video games grew 24 percent over the past five years, reaching a daily average of 1 hour, 13 minutes (Rideout, Foehr, and Roberts, 2010). Young people's use of computers grew 27 percent over the same time period, including an average of 17 minutes daily playing computer games and 22 minutes spent on social networking. Adult gaming is also growing rapidly (see Chapter 6).

While games designed purely for entertainment dominate the world of computer gaming, serious games are also emerging. In 2003, the Woodrow Wilson Center for International Scholars hosted a conference on serious games in Washington, DC, to explore how game-based simulation and learning technologies might enhance the performance of hospitals, high schools, and parks (see http://www.wilsoncenter.org/index.cfm?fuseaction=news. item&news_id=20313). More recently, a National Research Council committee (2010) observed that a game may be defined as "serious" by the player, a third party, or the game developer. For example, an overweight individual may use Wii for the serious purpose of losing weight, while another individual may play it simply for fun. A third party, such as a teacher, may use a commercial game about history as part of a class for the serious purpose of learning. Alternatively, a developer may create a game with a serious goal in mind while also seeking to retain enjoyable aspects of game play.

This report focuses primarily[1] on a particular type of serious game—games designed specifically to support science learning. As such, these games are designed to accurately model science or simulate scientific processes, and interactions within the virtual world of the game are governed by established scientific principles.

To more fully define and describe games and simulations, the committee presents several examples below.

---

[1]The report includes some discussion of commercial games as they relate to science learning and the potential for wider use of games designed for science learning.

Examples of Simulations and Games

Over the past three decades, developers have created a wide variety of simulations and games focused on science learning goals. To clarify this variety, the committee commissioned Clark and colleagues (2009) to categorize the major types of simulations and games, based on dimensions that may influence science learning.

Dimensions of Simulations

Clark et al. (2009) suggest that simulations used in science education can be classified along four primary dimensions: (1) the degree of user control, (2) the extent and nature of the surrounding guiding framework in which the simulations are embedded, (3) how information is represented, and (4) the nature of what is being modeled. These dimensions are illustrated in the following examples.

Degree of User Control. Although all simulations, in the committee's definition, allow user interaction, the degree of interaction varies. Some simulations focus the user, allowing him or her to control only a few specified variables, others allow greater control, and a few allow the user to fully control and program the underlying computer model or models.

One group of simulations can be described as "targeted," because they limit user choices to focus attention on key dynamics of interest. An example is the *Physics Education Technology* suite of simulations (*PhET*, see Box 1-2 and Figure 1-1). Other examples include small standalone simulations for physics learning, known as *Physlets,* and simulations embedded in larger online science learning environments.

Other simulations provide an intermediate level of user control. Because they allow more open-ended exploration, they are sometimes referred to as "sandbox" simulations (Clark et al., 2009).

Another type of simulation allows a high degree of user control. In these simulations, the typical user would modify variables to change outcomes in the simulation, while another user might access the underlying computer model and program it to change the basic rules underlying the simulation. For example, simulations developed using NetLogo (Wilensky, 1999)—a system of software and online modeling tools based on the easy-to-use Logo programming language—allow users to access and program the underlying computer model.

Representing yet another variation along the dimension of user control are networked participatory simulations controlled by multiple users. Each student (or small group of students) has a separate device, and data are exchanged among the devices; the student decisions and the information

BOX 1-2
Examples of Targeted Simulations in *PhET*

PhET (http://phet.colorado.edu), a large online library of simulations, includes suites of targeted simulations in the domains of physics, chemistry, biology, earth science, and mathematics. These simulations, which can be downloaded at no cost, are designed to allow teachers or students to use them with minimal prior training and to either supplement existing curricula or use them as the core of new inquiry projects. Research on the role of *PhET* simulations in student understanding of physics topics is discussed in Chapter 2.

Each simulation targets a specific science concept or set of concepts. For example, in the simulation shown in Figure 1-1, the learner can compare the pH of different virtual liquids to learn about acidity, alkalinity, and the concentration of solutes. When the learner makes a selection from a drop-down menu of solutions ranging from very alkaline (e.g., drain cleaner) to very acidic (e.g., battery acid), the simulation displays an image of the solution being poured into a beaker from a virtual tap. It also presents a graphical display of the amount of H_3O^+, OH^-, and H_2O in the solution (either in terms of concentration or in terms of the number of moles) and the pH of the solution on the pH scale. The learner can also add water to the beaker, increasing the volume of liquid and changing the pH of the solution, leading to changes in the graphical displays.

exchanged then reveal a pattern (Roschelle, 2003). Although each individual learner has limited control (similar to targeted simulations), the overall control is spread across the group. Some research suggests that participatory simulations motivate learners and enhance science learning (see Chapter 2).

Surrounding Framework. A second dimension of variation in simulations designed for science learning is whether, and to what extent, they are embedded in a larger framework. Some simulations, such as the *PhET* simulations described above, stand alone, allowing learners to access them with minimal curricular support or constraint. An instructor may freely integrate these simulations into the curriculum at whatever point or points he or she thinks would be most appropriate.

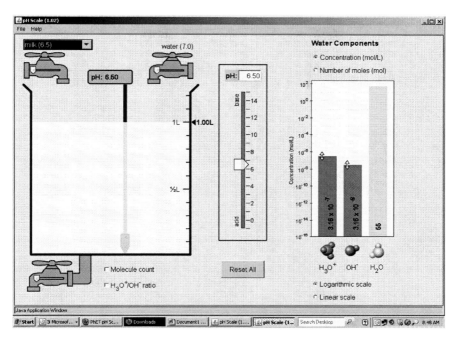

FIGURE 1-1 *Example of a targeted simulation in PhET.*
SOURCE: PhET Interactive Simulations, University of Colorado (http://phet.colorado. edu). Reprinted with permission.

Often, however, simulations are situated within a larger sequence of science instruction, referred to here as a curriculum unit. Although they provide the learner with more instructional support, curriculum units cannot be integrated as readily into existing curricula as standalone simulations can. They generally include multiple individual simulations that are integrated with other science teaching and learning activities, either online or in the classroom or the field. For example, in the *ThinkerTools* and *Model-Enhanced ThinkerTools* curriculum units, learners engage in an inquiry cycle that begins with a question about force and motion and includes developing a hypothesis, carrying out both real-world and simulated experiments to gather data, and using the data to evaluate their hypotheses and formulate a written law consistent with their data (see Chapter 2). Another example, the *Interactive Multimedia Exercises* (*IMMEX*), is an online library of simulated problem-solving activities that incorporates ongoing assessment of learner performance (see Chapter 5).

Representation of Information. Simulations also vary in the way they represent information. The learner may experience important variables or elements of the simulation in the form of alphanumeric text, graphs, symbols, or abstract icons. Although simulations of scientific phenomena typically include more than one of these different types of representations, they often rely heavily on only one or two types. Research on how different types of representations may influence science learning is ongoing (see Chapter 2).

Nature of What Is Modeled. A final dimension of simulations is what they model and how. Clark et al. (2009) propose that simulations can be classified into four subtypes along this dimension: (1) behavior-based models, (2) emergent models, (3) aggregate models, and (4) composite models of skills and processes.

Behavior-based models typically involve the user in manipulating the behavior of objects. For example, learners using the *Interactive Physics* simulation environment create objects of their choice, add behaviors (e.g., movement) and constraints (e.g., gravity and other forces), and observe the results. Emergent model simulations, such as those created with NetLogo, typically model complex systems. In these simulations, the learner controls simple decentralized interactions between many individual agents, leading to the emergence of a model of a complex scientific phenomenon. For example, in the *NetLogo Investigations in Electromagnetism* (*NIELS*) learning environment, the learner controls electrons and atoms (the agents) in a wire current to learn about electricity and resistance (see Chapter 2).

An aggregate model simulation allows the user to manipulate various objects or the computer code underlying them to model the aggregate-level behavior of a complex system. *STELLA*, an example of this type of simulation, has been used to model a variety of dynamic systems, including the relationships between predators and prey in an ecosystem, plant succession in a forest ecosystem, and carbon dioxide inflow and outflow into the atmosphere.

Composite models of processes and skills are simulated environments in which learners train for complex tasks. Originally developed for military training, such simulations are now used in medical and general education and training, allowing learners to simulate activities ranging from conducting a NASA mission to conducting a chemistry experiment (*ChemLab*) or dissecting a frog (e.g., *Froguts*).

Dimensions of Games

Clark et al. (2009) propose that games designed for science learning can be classified along four dimensions: (1) the science learning goal or goals targeted by the game, (2) the duration of the game, (3) the nature of participation in the game, and (4) the primary purpose of the game.

Science Learning Goals

Games and simulations have potential to advance multiple science learning goals, including motivation to learn science, conceptual understanding of science topics, science process skills, understanding of the nature of science, scientific discourse, and identification with science and science learning (these goals are discussed more fully in Chapter 2). Clark et al. (2009) propose that an important dimension of games is the science learning goal or goals they target. For example, the Minnesota Zoo and a small educational gaming company collaborated to create *WolfQuest Episode 1: Amethyst Mountain*. As a game intended for informal settings, one important goal is to be enjoyable, motivating interest in the game and attracting players. Underlying this goal is the goal of motivating players to learn about a specific scientific phenomenon—wolves and their ecosystems.[2] There is suggestive evidence that the game advances both goals.

In *WolfQuest*, the player takes on the role of a wolf to explore a swath of Yellowstone National Park. The game is designed as the educational equivalent of a multiplayer, first-person shooter[3] game. Players enter the game as wolf avatars, using their senses to track elk, pick out a weaker elk, and then hunt it down. They may have to defend a carcass against grizzly bears and other competitors. Players can go it alone or join a pack with their friends—but if they do that, they have to learn how to cooperate with other members of the pack.

Players' responses to the game have exceeded the developers' expectations (Schaller et al., 2009). About 4,000 people downloaded the game in the first hour after it was launched in 2007; since then, over 400,000 people in 200 countries have downloaded the game. A moderated online forum supports discussion about wolves, their ecosystems, and places to go for more information.

When Goldman, Koepfler, and Yocco (2009) conducted a web-based survey of players, most respondents indicated that they had sought out more information about wolves and their environments, suggesting that the game motivates interest in science learning. Analysis of players' self-reported knowledge of wolves, their behaviors, and habitats before and after playing *WolfQuest* suggests that the game has a positive impact on conceptual understanding of wolves. In addition, a slight majority of respondents reported that they had engaged in science processes—such as model-based reason-

---

[2]Chapter 2 provides a much more extensive discussion of the research on the effectiveness of various games and simulations in advancing science learning goals. The extended example here illustrates one dimension of games.

[3]In a first-person shooter game, the player experiences simulated combat through the eyes of a protagonist armed with a gun or projectile weapon.

ing, testing and prediction, and collecting and using data—to respond to challenges in the game.

Duration of Participation. The second dimension categorizes the duration of game participation, mirroring a distinction in the commercial gaming world between short-term "casual games" and longer, often narrative-based, experiences, like those in *WolfQuest*. In this dimension, Clark et al. (2009) classified games into three types: (1) short-duration games, (2) fixed-duration games organized with specific start and stop times, and (3) ongoing participation games in which players become members of a persistent ongoing community in or around the game.

Short-duration games are designed to be played in only a few minutes, but players may play such games—or variations of them—repeatedly. These casual games are typically accessed from the Internet and may be played on handheld devices, such as cell phones, as well as on computers.

For three decades, many casual video games have organized their play around core physics concepts, allowing players to develop tacit, intuitive understandings of physics. Researchers developed the short-duration game *SURGE* with the goal of supporting players not only to develop these intuitive concepts, but also to connect them with more formal understandings of the motion of objects and Newton's laws. *SURGE* incorporates formal physics ideas into the narrative, which revolves around navigating a player-controlled spaceship through a series of two-dimensional challenge levels. Learners use the arrow keys to apply impulses to the spaceship, thereby modifying its motion. They must apply one or more physics principles to achieve the objectives of the game, thinking carefully about navigation decisions to manage their limited fuel resources, avoid collisions, and minimize travel time (see Chapter 2 for discussion of the game's effectiveness for learning). Similar short-duration, casual games designed for science learning include *Supercharged*, *London Museum's Launchball*, *ImmuneAttack*, and *Weatherlings*.

River City is an example of a fixed-duration game integrated with other forms of science instruction in a middle school curriculum unit (see Box 1-3).

Along the dimension of duration, a third group of games is persistent. One example is *Whyville*, a multiplayer online game for preteens and teens with a predominately female player base of about 5 million (Mayo, 2009a). Players leave and return to the game at will over long durations of time (months or years), creating a persistent, virtual community.

The *Whyville* player enters a web-based cartoonlike two-dimensional world and is free to choose games and activities designed for both entertainment and learning. As in many other games, the player creates an avatar to represent her in the game (see Figure 1-2). The avatar chats with other players (text appears in balloons above the avatars), earns clams by completing

BOX 1-3
River City

River City is structured around visits to the virtual world of River City that can be completed within a typical science class period of 45 minutes. For example, in one study, students spent approximately 12 science class periods using the curriculum unit, including 2 periods devoted to presurveys, 6 class periods visiting *River City,* and 4 days devoted to team design work and interpretation and whole-class discussion led by the teacher (Ketelhut, 2007).

In *River City*, students travel back in time to help the mayor of River City figure out why the residents have fallen ill. The virtual 19th century industrial city is concentrated around a river that runs from the mountains downstream to a dump and a bog. Students' avatars can interact with computer-based agents who are residents of the city, digital objects (e.g., historical photographs), and the avatars of other students. They encounter various stimuli, such as mosquitoes buzzing and people coughing, that provide clues as to possible causes of illness, and they can use objects in the world. For example, they can click on the virtual microscope and use it to visually examine water samples.

Students work in teams of three or four to develop and test hypotheses about why residents are ill. However, each student sits individually at a computer, communicating with teammates through chat. Three different illnesses (water-borne, air-borne, and insect-borne) are integrated with historical, social, and geographic content, allowing students to develop and practice the inquiry skills involved in disentangling multicausal problems embedded in a complex environment (see Chapter 2 for discussion of research on the game's effectiveness for science learning). *River City's* approach of engaging the player in science inquiry projects in three-dimensional immersive worlds is shared by a number of other single and multiplayer science games, including *WolfQuest, Quest Atlantis* (described in Chapter 2), and *Resilient Planet* (described in Chapter 4).

FIGURE 1-2 *Example of an avatar in Whyville.*
SOURCE: Numedeon, Inc. Reprinted with permission.

activities, and may spend the clams to refine and enhance her appearance and her personal space. Researchers have studied how the introduction of an epidemic of "Whypox" into this persistent game influenced learning about how disease is transmitted (see Chapters 2 and 3).

Nature of Participation. Players participate in most of the games described thus far through a virtual world, which may range from Yellowstone National Park (*WolfQuest*) to a historic American city (*River City*) to outer space (*SURGE*). A different group of games engages the player in the real world, supplementing action in this world with digital information. Clark et al. (2009) refer to these as augmented reality games.

In MIT-augmented reality (MITAR) games, multiple players use location-aware handheld computers that add a digital layer of information to the game that happens in the real world, frequently outdoors. Players navigate the physical space and work collaboratively to explore and solve complex problems during the game. MITAR games include *Savannah,* in which players become lions who prowl in real space, and *TimeLab 2100*, in which players merge observations of the real world made outdoors with information about climate change from their handheld computers (Massachusetts Institute of Technology, 2010).

Purpose of the Game. Clark et al.'s (2009) fourth dimension of variation in games is the intended purpose of the game. They propose that games can be classified as (1) fully recreational games that are designed for entertainment purposes (e.g., *World of Warcraft*); (2) serious games that maintain many design elements of recreational games but have a more purposeful curricular focus, such as *Resilient Planet*; (3) serious games designed for use in classroom settings, such as *SURGE;* and (4) assessment games that are designed primarily as a vehicle for assessing existing knowledge and understanding, rather than as a learning platform. This report focuses primarily on categories 2 and 3—serious games designed for science learning.

Clark et al. (2009) note that these dimensions are not mutually exclusive, nor are they exhaustive. Any given game may contain elements from multiple dimensions while weighting toward one in particular.

The Potential of Simulations and Games for Learning

Simulations and games appear to have great potential to address the science education challenges identified at the beginning of this chapter. A growing body of research is beginning to illuminate how people learn science and how best to support that learning (National Research Council, 2005b, 2007a). This research indicates that developing proficiency in science is much more than knowing facts. Students need to learn how facts and ideas are related to each other within conceptual frameworks. Although good teaching can facilitate this process, developing conceptual understanding of science is difficult and takes time. Engaging students in the processes of science—including talk and argument, modeling and representation, and learning from investigations—aids development of proficiency. These science processes (often called science inquiry) motivate students by fostering their natural curiosity about the world around them, encouraging them to persist through difficulty to master complex science concepts. New science teaching approaches that carefully integrate science processes with other forms of instruction and target clear learning goals have been shown to increase interest in science, enhance scientific reasoning, and increase mastery of the targeted concepts (National Research Council, 2005b).

However, students have difficulty with all aspects of inquiry, from posing a research question to designing an investigation to building and revising scientific models (National Research Council, 2005b). They often become confused when allowed to engage in open-ended investigations and require guidance to make meaning from these activities (Mayer, 2004). Students' difficulties, in turn, place new demands on science teachers for deep content knowledge and effective teaching strategies. States and school districts have been slow to adopt inquiry approaches to science instruction because of these challenges and because current state science standards and assessments emphasizing coverage of many science content topics may leave little time for science process activities.[4] Practical and logistical constraints, such as a lack of laboratory facilities and supplies or a long distance from outdoor learning sites or science museums, can also slow movement toward this promising new approach.

Computer simulations and games can support the new, inquiry-based approaches to science instruction, providing virtual laboratories or field learning experiences that overcome practical and logistical constraints to student investigations. They can allow learners to visualize, explore, and formulate scientific explanations for scientific phenomena that would otherwise be impossible to observe and manipulate. They can help learners mentally link abstract representations of a scientific phenomenon (for example, equations) with the invisible processes[5] underlying the phenomenon and the learner's own observations (Linn et al., 2010). Simulations and games provide intermediate models that students may be able to understand more readily than more detailed but more complex models. For example, Hmelo-Silver et al. (2008) propose that use of a simulation allowed middle school science students who were studying an aquatic ecosystem to look beyond the surface structures and functions they could see when an aquarium served as a physical model. They suggest that interacting with the simulation allowed students to mentally create connections between the macro-level fish reproduction and the micro-level nutrification processes in the aquatic ecosystem.

As digital technologies, both simulations and games appeal to young people who are increasingly immersed in all forms of digital media (Rideout, Foehr, and Roberts, 2010). K-12 students responding to national surveys indicate that they would like to learn science and mathematics through simulations and video games (Partnership for Reform in Science and Mathematics, 2005; Project Tomorrow and PASCO Scientific, 2008).

Games that successfully integrate fun and learning may have especially great potential to motivate young people for science learning, supporting inquiry approaches in the context of the popular activity of computer gaming. Games can spark high levels of engagement, encourage repetition and

---

[4]The National Research Council is currently developing a new framework for science education standards that emphasizes integrated learning of science content and process skills.

[5]These underlying processes can be invisible due to time scale (too fast or slow to perceive), size (too big or too small to be seen), or form (e.g., radio waves).

practice, and motivate learners with challenges and rapid feedback (Clark et al., 2009). Games that embed ongoing assessment and feedback offer the possibility of individualizing instruction to match the progress and learning needs of the individual learner (see Chapter 5). Such games can motivate learning at various times and places, blurring the boundaries between learning in and out of school (see Chapters 3 and 4). Increasing learning time, focusing instruction toward individual learning needs and opportunities, and providing ongoing formative feedback have been shown to support learning generally and science learning specifically (National Research Council, 2000, 2004). Recognizing this potential, blue-ribbon panels have recently called for increased use of games to boost U.S. students' science learning (Federation of American Scientists, 2007; Thai et al., 2009).

Limits of the Research

Research that could help achieve the potential of simulations and games to improve science achievement is limited. When compared with subject areas such as reading and mathematics, there is relatively little research evidence on the effectiveness of simulations and games for learning. As in any newly-emerging field, there is a tension between development and research. Creative game designers unfamiliar with education research focus on developing new games and rarely study the effectiveness of their products, whereas cognitive scientists may create a game or simulation for the specific purpose of investigating its effects on learning.[6]

To date, the majority of research on learning through interaction with games and simulations has been at a proof of concept stage, meaning that researchers have sought to prove that a functioning game or simulation can engage students in inquiry, enhance motivation, or advance another science learning goal (Clark et al., 2009). Only a few studies clearly articulate the learning goal of the simulation or game; the theory of action about how the goal will be advanced; and the measures, analyses, and data used to assess learners' progress toward the goal. Most studies lack control groups, making it difficult to conclude that the game or simulation caused any learning gains observed among the study participants. In addition, researchers often develop and test curriculum units that integrate simulations and games with other science learning activities, but do not distinguish the unique effects of the game or simulation from the overall effects of the curriculum unit.

Another challenge is that researchers from different disciplines have

---

[6]Although they are less knowledgeable about research than cognitive scientists or other academic developers of simulations or games, commercial game publishers have expertise in marketing and distributing their products that academic developers often lack (see Chapter 6).

used various methods to study the effectiveness of games and simulations in advancing science learning goals. Common definitions and terminology are lacking, not only because of the variety of disciplinary perspectives and science learning goals, but also because of rapid evolution in the design and technology of games and simulations. All of these factors make it difficult to integrate findings across studies and build a coherent base of evidence (see Chapter 2 for further discussion).

CONCLUSIONS

The science achievement of U.S. elementary and secondary students is uneven and has not improved greatly over the past decade. This trend is worrisome, because solving pressing societal issues will require both a scientifically informed citizenry and a robust scientific and technical workforce. Students' uneven achievement is caused partly by current science education approaches, which often fail to motivate students for science learning.

A growing body of research indicates that engaging students in science processes (inquiry) can motivate and support science learning. However, because inquiry approaches can be difficult for students, teachers, and schools, they are rarely implemented. Computer simulations and games have great potential to catalyze and support inquiry-based approaches to science instruction, overcoming curricular and logistical barriers. Computer simulations and games appeal to young people who enjoy interacting with computers and playing digital games outside of school.

Conclusion: *Computer simulations and games have great potential to catalyze and support inquiry-based approaches to science instruction, overcoming current barriers to widespread use of these approaches. As digital technologies, computer simulations and games appeal to young people who are increasingly immersed in digital media throughout the day.*

Simulations and games share several important characteristics. Both are both based on computer models that simulate natural, engineered, or invented phenomena and most games incorporate simulations as part of their basic architecture. At the same time, each technology has unique features.

Conclusion: *Games and simulations lie along a continuum. Both are based on computer models and allow user interactions, yet each also has unique features. Simulations are dynamic computer models that allow users to explore the implications of manipulating or modifying parameters within them. Games are played in informal contexts for fun, incorporate explicit goals and rules, and provide feedback on the player's progress. In a game, the player's actions affect the state of play.*

For over 30 years, developers have created a variety of simulations for the purpose of supporting science learning. More recently, researchers and game designers have begun to create games that aim to integrate science learning with enjoyment.

Conclusion: *Developers and researchers have created a wide variety of simulations and games that vary along a number of dimensions, such as the degree of user control they provide, how information is represented, the science learning goals targeted, duration, and intended purpose.*

In this chapter, the committee used the dimensions of simulations and games identified by Clark et al. (2009) to elaborate upon its definition of simulations and games and illustrate the variety of simulations and games. However, the committee has questions about the relationship of some of these dimensions to science learning. For example, the committee agrees with Clark et al. (2009) that the degree of user control in a simulation may influence its capacity to support learning, but notes that the degree of user control may be an important dimension influencing science learning in a game as well. In addition, the committee questions whether the duration of a game strongly influences its effectiveness for science learning. Research indicates that the short-duration game *SURGE* can help students learn physics concepts (Clark et al., 2010), and the amount of time students spend playing the fixed-duration game *River City* may vary, as students have requested and been given access to play the game after school and during lunch hours, increasing play time (see Chapter 3). This extended time is elicited by another attribute of the game—its narrative, or story, and its related capacity to immerse the player in the simulated environment.

The question of which attributes of simulations and games are important for student learning can be addressed only by reviewing the available research. The following chapter provides such a review, along with a preliminary list of design features of simulations and games that appear to influence learning.

2

Learning with Simulations and Games

This chapter discusses research evidence related to the use of simulations and games for science learning. The first section presents the committee's framework for its review of the research, identifying five science learning goals. The next two sections review and discuss research on the effectiveness of simulations and games in advancing each of these goals. The fourth section synthesizes research findings related to a set of design features that appear to influence the effectiveness of simulations and games in supporting learning, and the fifth section describes limitations of the research. The chapter concludes with a summary of key findings—both about the effectiveness of simulations and games and about the state of the research.

LEARNING GOALS

The committee views science learning as a complex, multifaceted process that involves not only mastering science concepts, but also skills in designing and carrying out scientific investigations and feelings and attitudes toward science. To identify the learning goals of simulations and games, the committee drew on a previous definition of informal science learning (National Research Council, 2009). That study identified six interwoven strands as valued goals of informal science learning:

Strand 1: Experience excitement, interest, and motivation to learn about phenomena in the natural and physical world (motivation).

Strand 2: Come to generate, understand, remember, and use concepts, explanations, arguments, models, and facts related to science (conceptual understanding).

This strand emphasizes understanding of fundamental concepts rather than memorization of unconnected facts.

Strand 3: Manipulate, test, explore, predict, question, observe, and make sense of the natural and physical world (science process skills).
This may include making observations, formulating a research question, developing a hypothesis (perhaps in the form of a model), using a range of methods to gather data, data analysis, and confirmation or revision of the hypothesis.

Strand 4: Reflect on science as a way of knowing; on processes, concepts, and institutions of science, as well as on the learners' own process of learning about phenomena (understanding of the nature of science).

Strand 5: Participate in scientific activities and learning practices with others, using scientific language and tools (scientific discourse).
This strand flows out of the notion that science takes place in a community that shares norms, practices, and a common language and that learners should be introduced to these norms and practices as they engage with science.

Strand 6: Think about themselves as science learners and develop an identity as someone who knows about, uses, and sometimes contributes to science (identity).
This strand may be reflected in one's ability to effectively apply scientific knowledge to life situations (e.g., health decisions) or at work, whether or not one works in a science-related job.

These six strands of informal science learning are closely intertwined and mutually supportive. They reflect the theory that mastery of science concepts and understanding of the nature of science are supported and accelerated when students engage in the processes of science. This theory is supported by a growing body of research evidence (National Research Council, 2005b, 2007). The strands are also based on a growing body of research that illuminates the importance of motivation, the social and cultural context, and feelings of identity and self-efficacy in supporting learning generally and science learning in particular (National Research Council, 2005b, 2007, 2009). The strands are well aligned with other recent theories of how people learn, such as theories that view education as a process of preparing for future learning and problem solving (Bransford and Schwartz, 1999; Schwartz, Bransford, and Sears, 2005).

Because science process skills and understanding of the nature of science are especially closely related, the committee merged them, reducing the number of learning goals from six to five. These five goals provided a valuable framework for the committee's deliberations about the use of gaming and simulations to support science learning and they serve as a template in the following review of the research. Although the review is organized by separate goals, it illuminates the capacity of some simulations and games to simultaneously advance multiple science learning goals.

EFFECTIVENESS OF SIMULATIONS

The available research on the effectiveness of simulations for learning is more extensive and stronger than the research on games. However, both simulations and games are relatively young learning technologies, and developers have focused primarily on design, with less attention to research. Some studies have examined how a simulation affects a single group of learners without a control group of similar learners who receive science instruction targeted to the same learning goal but without the simulation. Other studies compare one or more groups of learners who interact with different versions of a simulation. In these studies, the lack of control of other variables that may influence learning makes it unclear whether any reported learning gains can be attributed to the simulation (or one version of it) alone.

A related challenge is that simulations are often embedded within a larger curriculum unit, making it difficult to disentangle the effects of the simulation(s). Ma and Nickerson (2006) discuss this problem in their review of the literature comparing hands-on, virtual, and remote laboratories in undergraduate science education. They found that investigators often confounded the effects of many different factors and perhaps over-attributed learning gains to simulations or other learning technologies.

The research also includes a few studies focusing on the goal of conceptual understanding, in which investigators used control or comparison groups or other elements of the study design to try to limit the influence of other variables. These studies provide stronger evidence that simulations are effective. It is important to keep in mind the strengths and weaknesses of study designs when reviewing research findings.

Overall, the research provides promising evidence that the use of simulations can enhance conceptual understanding in science and moderate evidence that simulations can motivate interest in science and science learning. There is more limited or no evidence that simulations advance the other science learning goals defined above.

Motivation

Research over the past three decades indicates that simulations can encourage learners to experience excitement, interest, and motivation to learn about phenomena in the natural and physical world (Clark et al, 2009). Building on these findings, more recent research indicates that simulations and simulation-based curriculum units motivate learners by providing them with authentic, interesting tasks and contexts (e.g., Adams et al., 2008a, 2008b; Cognition and Technology Group at Vanderbilt, 1990; Edelson, Gordin, and Pea, 1999). Some examples follow.

In a study of the *PhET* suite of simulations (see Box 1-2), Adams et al. (2008a) conducted over 200 structured interviews with 89 undergraduate student volunteers, focusing on 52 simulations targeting different physics concepts. For each simulation, the authors interviewed a diverse group of four to six students with equal numbers of male and female students and a representative share of minority students. The volunteers (typically non-science majors) included students who had not yet received formal instruction on the topics covered by the simulations. Trained interviewers with advanced physics knowledge asked students to describe their understanding of an idea or concept before seeing the simulation and allowed them to revise their answers while interacting with the simulation or afterward; they also asked students to think aloud as they freely explored the simulations.

The results suggest that the simulations' effectiveness in motivating learners was closely related to their effectiveness in supporting conceptual understanding. The authors found that a *PhET* simulation can be highly engaging and effective for mastering physics concepts, but only if the student's interaction with the simulation is directed by the student's own questioning—a process they refer to as "engaged exploration." Through this process, most study participants were able to accurately describe the concepts covered in the simulation and apply the concepts to correctly predict behaviors in the simulation. The participants also frequently volunteered correct predictions or explanations about related phenomena. Although the study did not include a control group, the authors described the study participants' level of conceptual understanding as much greater than the level typically reached by students taught about these concepts in a physics course. They also noted that study participants regularly reported playing with several simulations for fun during their leisure time—suggesting that the simulations are motivating and engaging.

In another study, Edelson et al. (1999) found that incorporating the challenge of global warming in the *WorldWatcher* visualization-based curriculum unit enhanced motivation for learning. The researchers used an informal evaluation approach in a rapid cycle of iterative design and testing of the unit, seeking a design that would motivate students to engage and persist in the investigations included within the unit. Formative evaluation of early versions of the curriculum unit led to the decision to incorporate the challenge of global warming. In a pilot test of the revised curriculum unit in three schools, the authors observed and videotaped students interacting with the visualization and obtained teacher and student journals and informal teacher feedback. The data indicated that students found four aspects of the global warming challenge motivating: It was familiar, it had potential direct implications for students, the policy issues appealed to students' sense of fairness, and it was a subject of current scientific debate and controversy.

Both Edelson, Gordin, and Pea (1999) and Adams et al. (2008a, 2008b) caution that encouraging students' interest, engagement, and motivation is a very challenging task for the designer of a simulation or simulation-based learning environment.

Klopfer, Yoon, and Rivas (2004) studied two participatory simulations, comparing the relative ability of two different technology platforms to motivate students to persist through the difficulties of inquiry learning incorporated within these simulations. Students from two Boston area high schools—one public ($N = 71$ in four classes) and one private ($N = 117$ in six classes)—played *Live Long and Prosper,* a game focusing on Mendelian genetics. Students at one private middle school ($N = 82$ in five classes) played the *Virus* game, which simulates transmission of a virus. Within each school, half of the classes were randomly assigned to use either wearable computers or Palm Pilots while participating in the simulation.

Data from pre- and post-activity questionnaires revealed no significant differences between schools, classes, or technology in students' ratings of engagement. The pooled data showed that students felt like they had fun and expressed a strong interest in playing other participatory simulation games. After playing the games, students felt more strongly that they could learn a lot about science from games. They also highly rated their learning about science content and experimental design and expressed strong agreement with the statement that the technology used positively impacted their learning.

Conceptual Understanding

Most studies of simulations focus on the goal of enhancing conceptual understanding (de Jong, 2009; Quellmalz, Timms, and Schneider, 2009). They provide promising evidence that simulations can help students generate, understand, remember, and use science concepts, particularly when they are supported by other forms of instruction within a larger curriculum unit (Clark et al., 2009).

Many studies have examined the potential of simulations to help students replace their intuitive alternative explanations of natural phenomena with scientifically correct explanations. For example, Meir et al. (2005) hypothesized that students' deep-rooted misconceptions about diffusion and osmosis might be partly due to their inability to see and explore these processes at the molecular level. To investigate this, they developed *OsmoBeaker,* a set of two simulated laboratories, one focusing on diffusion and the other on osmosis. Each laboratory included a series of simulated experiments and a workbook. To test *OsmoBeaker*, the researchers recruited student volunteers from 11 Boston-area colleges, ranging from large, well-known universities to small community colleges. Among the volunteers, 83 percent were freshmen or sophomores and 71 percent were women. Eighty-four percent had received instruction on osmosis in an introductory college biology class, and most of the others had studied osmosis in high school biology. At least half had completed a wet lab on osmosis.

Each participant met with a researcher for a 2-hour session and was financially compensated. The participant first read a description of osmosis and diffusion, then completed a written pretest, and then worked through the simulated laboratory experiments for about 45-60 minutes before completing a posttest. Both the pretest and posttest focused on alternative conceptions of diffusion and osmosis. The authors tested the diffusion laboratory on 15 students and the osmosis laboratory on 31 students. On the diffusion laboratory, 13 out of 15 students showed statistically significant gains from pretest to posttest, and on the osmosis laboratory, 23 of 31 students demonstrated statistically significant gains. Based on these results and interviews with study participants, the authors concluded that the simulated experiments helped students overcome several common alternative conceptions about diffusion and osmosis.

Although this study lacked a comparison group, all study participants had received previous instruction on diffusion, osmosis, or both prior to engaging with the simulation. This gives greater strength to the conclusion by Meir et al. (2005, p. 245) that "the improvements observed after the computer laboratories are above and beyond what students learn by reading or listening to material on the topic."

Another strand of research on the use of simulations to address alternative conceptions focuses NetLogo simulations (Wilensky, 1999). Sengupta and Wilensky (2008a, 2008b, 2009) studied *NetLogo Investigations in Electromagnetism* (*NIELS*). This sequence of simulations allows learners to manipulate representations of electrons at the microscopic level to help them understand the behavior of electric current moving through a wire at the macroscopic level.

Sengupta and Wilensky (2008a) studied a group of fifth and seventh graders who interacted with a revised version of *NIELS*. The revised version framed the motion of electrons in terms of a process of accumulation inside the positively-charged end of a battery—a change designed to address intuitive conceptions about electric current that appeared, from earlier research, to pose a barrier to the correct scientific understanding. Two science classes of 20 students each worked with the revised version of the simulation during one 45-minute class period, recording their observations in detail on log sheets. The researchers analyzed the log sheets and interviewed a sample of four randomly selected students within each class to gain insight into students' thinking.

Over 90 percent of students in both classes using the revised version of *NIELS* displayed correct reasoning about the behavior of electrons in an electric current. The performance of these novice learners was not statistically different from the performance of 12th graders who had used the pilot version of *NIELS*. The authors concluded that the reframing of the motion of electrons helped the younger students build on their naïve ideas about electricity to develop a correct understanding.

A related study of middle school students suggests that their interaction with NetLogo-based simulations enhanced their understanding of statistical mechanics, a topic that is traditionally taught using equation-based representations in college-level physics (Wilensky, 2003).

To address students' alternative conceptions in chemistry, researchers developed *ChemCollective*, a collection of simulated laboratories and other learning activities (Yaron et al., 2010). Cuadros and Yaron (2007) investigated the use of the virtual laboratories, assigned as homework, in a second-semester chemistry class of 144 students. Students completed a pretest focusing on chemistry concepts, and also took three midterm exams and a final exam focusing on the same concepts; the homework assignments were graded. The authors found that the homework grades accounted for 24 percent of the variation in exam scores, suggesting that engaging in science processes with the virtual laboratories increased students' conceptual understanding. In addition, the lack of a significant relationship between the homework grades and the pretest scores suggests that virtual laboratory activities developed additional understanding beyond what students brought to the class.

In one of the few controlled studies of simulations, Evans, Yaron, and Leinhardt (2008) studied the simulated laboratories, integrated with other forms of instruction in an online stoichiometry course. The course included an overarching narrative designed to motivate student learning, a variety of virtual laboratory activities, and rapid feedback during laboratory practice. The comparison course was a text-based study guide addressing the same topics presented in the online course. Both the online and text-based courses were designed for self-study, because all first-semester chemistry students were required to study stoichiometry on their own time in preparation for a mastery exam.

Entering college freshmen volunteers were randomly assigned to either the online class or the text-based class. A total of 45 students (27 male and 18 female) completed either the online course (21 students) or the text-only course (24 students) over a period of 10 to 24 days. After the end date of the study, participants completed a proctored test of stoichiometry concepts and procedures on campus. Statistical analysis revealed a significant gain in test scores among the online group when compared with the text-only group. However, regression analysis of posttest scores indicated that only 6 percent of the variability in performance was explained by treatment (i.e., participation in either the online or text-based course). Among the students in the online course, nearly 40 percent of the variation in posttest scores was related to the degree to which the student interacted with the virtual laboratory. Although the study does not demonstrate that simulations are more effective than other forms of science instruction, it provides further evidence that simulations can help students master science concepts by engaging them in science processes.

Recent Syntheses of Research on Simulations

Linn and Eylon (in press) synthesized findings from three types of studies: (1) laboratory investigations that compare static diagrams to dynamic simulations, (2) classroom comparison studies that compare simulation-supported instruction with typical text-based instruction, and (3) classroom studies of the use of simulations without comparison groups that use a pretest-posttest design. The laboratory-based studies generally indicated that well-designed simulations are more effective for learning than static diagrams, but the studies had mixed results, with effect sizes ranging from –0.5 to 1.76. The authors' analysis of classroom comparison studies found that simulations are more effective than typical instruction, with consistently positive effects averaging 0.49 across the studies. Analysis of the third group of studies found that simulations had a large positive effect, averaging 1.17. However, the authors note that these studies lack control groups and sometimes confound the larger instructional design with the specific effects of the simulation.

Noting these mixed findings about the effectiveness of simulations, Linn et al. (2010) identify three design principles to improve learning outcomes. First, simulations should minimize irrelevant cognitive demand to avoid distracting students from the primary learning goal. Second, simulations should be presented in a personally meaningful scientific context, allowing students to draw on what they already know, ask more effective questions, and recognize unlikely findings. Third, simulations should be embedded in supportive instruction, such as guidance on how to conduct simulated experiments. For example, Chang (2009) compared two approaches to learning about heat and temperature, in which students either read about how to conduct virtual experiments or critiqued the experiments of others before conducting their own virtual experiments. Pretests and posttests indicated that both groups of students made considerable progress in understanding thermal conductivity and equilibrium; however, the critique group had larger learning gains than the other group. In addition, the critique group was more successful than the other group in responding to an assessment item that asked students to plan a second trial after being given a research question and the results of a first trial related to the research question.

In another recent synthesis, Scalise et al. (2009) identified 79 articles that examined the use of simulations, including virtual laboratories, in grades 6-12 and included reports of measured learning outcomes. The most frequent research design, used in slightly over half of the studies, was to compare results from pretests and posttests of student learning on goals and objectives. Approximately 40 percent of the studies also, or alternatively, used a quasi-experimental research design, comparing a treatment group that received the simulations with a group that received another type of science instruction not involving virtual laboratories or simulations. In addition, just over 15 percent of the articles used literature synthesis of results from other studies, 10 percent were qualitative case studies, and the remaining 10 percent used other approaches. None of the 79 studies used a true experimental research design, with random assignment of participants to either a treatment group or a control group.

Across these 79 studies, slightly over half (53 percent) reported gains in learning among those taught with the simulations, about 25 percent found mixed outcomes in which some groups showed learning gains but others did not, 18 percent found gains under the right conditions, and approximately 4 percent reported no gain in learning. Scalise et al. (2009) note that many of the studies that lacked comparison groups were designed to quickly obtain feedback from students or teachers for the purpose of developing a simulation product and caution that the reported learning gains might not align well with findings that would result from more systematic research designs.

Conceptual Understanding in Domains Outside Science

Simulations for military training have demonstrated effectiveness in enhancing the conceptual understanding and related skills needed to perform specific jobs; cost-effectiveness is a key measure of success (Fletcher, 2009a, 2009b). For example, *SHERLOCK* is a simulation-based training system designed to prepare technicians to solve electronics problems when maintaining avionics equipment. Lesgold et al. (1992) estimated that a trainee who spent 20 hours interacting with the system developed problem-solving ability equivalent to that of an avionics technician with 4 years of learning on the job.

Another example focuses on the sophisticated knowledge of oceanography needed by Navy personnel who use advanced sonar to detect submarines. The *Interactive Multisensor Analysis Training* (*IMAT*) simulation-based training system presents trainees with a comprehensive range of virtual situations representing the required knowledge and skill. Wulfeck, Wetzel-Smith, and Baker (2007) found that *IMAT* graduates scored higher on an assessment of oceanography knowledge and skills than fleet personnel with 3 to 10 years of experience, and *IMAT*-trained officers performed as well on an assessment of search planning as officers with 4 to 6 years of experience in planning sonar searches for submarines.

Science Process Skills and Understanding of the Nature of Science

The goal of developing students' ability to manipulate, test, explore, predict, question, observe, and make sense of the natural and physical world (science process skills) is closely related to the goal that students reflect on science as a way of knowing; on processes, concepts, and institutions of science; and on their own science learning (understanding of the nature of science). Although simulations and simulation-based curriculum units often engage students in selected science processes (see Box 1-2), only a few studies have focused on—or directly assessed—their potential to advance these two learning goals.

One study that that specifically examined science process skills focused on *ThinkerTools,* a simulation-based curriculum unit addressing Newton's laws of motion (White and Frederiksen, 1998). In the curriculum, students formulate a research question, generate alternative hypotheses and predictions, design and carry out both real-world and simulated experiments, analyze the resulting data, construct a conceptual model with scientific laws that would predict and explain what they found, and apply their model to different situations thereby leading to new research questions.

White and Frederiksen (1998) tested two different versions of *Thinkertools,* one with formative assessments integrated throughout, designed to encourage students to self-assess and reflect on core aspects of inquiry and their own learning, and another without these self-assessment prompts. The researchers implemented the curriculum unit in 12 urban seventh-, eighth-, and ninth-grade classrooms, incorporating it in daily science instruction over a period of about 10.5 weeks. The classes included 343 students taught by 3 teachers, and two-thirds of the students were minorities. Classrooms were randomly assigned to either the reflective self-assessment version or the control version.

The researchers evaluated understanding of scientific investigations using a pre-post inquiry test and compared gains in scores for the reflective self-assessment classes with gains in scores in control classrooms. Results were also broken out by students categorized as high and low achieving, based on performance on a standardized test conducted before the intervention. The test results showed gains for all students in their understanding of scientific investigations, and the self-assessment classes exhibited greater gains. This was especially true for low-achieving students.

ThinkerTools also appeared to advance conceptual understanding, as measured by a posttest focusing on force and motion. On one difficult test item that had been included in an earlier study, the middle school students performed significantly better, on average, than did a comparison group of 40 high school students who had completed a high school-level physics class. In terms of the goal of motivation, student surveys conducted before and after participation in the curriculum unit indicated that students felt more positive about their ability to learn and understand science following their interactions with *ThinkerTools*.

More recently, Schwarz and White (2005) developed and studied the *Model-Enhanced ThinkerTools (METT)* curriculum unit, focusing on three learning goals: (1) science process (inquiry) skills, (2) understanding of the nature of science (specifically, knowledge of models and modeling), and (3) conceptual understanding of physics. The *METT* curriculum unit extended *ThinkerTools* by allowing students to create, evaluate, and discuss computer models of their ideas about force and motion, and it included instruction on the nature of models and modeling.

Schwarz and White (2005) tested *METT* in four seventh-grade science classes in an urban school that met daily for 45 minutes over the course of 10.5 weeks. Approximately 44 percent of the school's students were black, 31 percent were white, 13 percent were Asian, and 11 percent were Hispanic. Additionally, 34 percent of students qualified for free or reduced-price meals, and 20 percent came from families who received Aid for Dependent Children. Study participants' scores on the Individual Test of Academic Skills varied, with a median percentile score of 66—higher than the median score of 60 on the Comprehensive Test of Basic Skills among students involved in the earlier test of *ThinkerTools*.

Student scores on three written pretests and posttests—a modeling assessment, an inquiry test, and a conceptual physics test—showed significant gains. Comparison of *METT* students' gains in inquiry and physics concepts with those of the prior *ThinkerTools* students revealed no significant difference overall. However, the *METT* students performed better on one section of the inquiry test focusing on conclusions, which suggested that the emphasis on modeling helped them to draw appropriate conclusions from their experimental data. Finally, analysis of *METT* students' test results suggested that their gains in knowledge of modeling (a dimension of understanding of the nature of science) and science process skills supported their gains in physics knowledge.

Two studies of participatory simulations examined development of science process skills. In a pilot study by Colella (2000), urban high school biology students wearing small portable computers acted as agents in a dynamic simulation of the transmission of a virus in the closed system of the classroom. The class consisted mainly of tenth-grade students, who were described by their teacher as traditionally poor performers in science. Sixteen students, seven girls and nine boys, along with their teacher, participated in the activities.

The author's analysis of video and audio recordings of the students as they engaged in the simulation over the course of six class sessions indicated that they advanced in science process skills. After exploring and observing the transmission of the virus in the first few sessions, they developed hypotheses about how the virus spread and then began to systematically collect data to confirm or deny their hypotheses. By the final session, they could articulate the underlying rules of the simulation.

In another study, Klopfer, Yoon, and Um (2005) examined a virus simulation that was similar to that studied by Colella (2000) and *Live Long and Prosper*, a simulation of Mendelian genetic inheritance. The fifth- and seventh-grade students gained an understanding of the importance of several scientific practices, such as repeated testing and revision of a hypothesis; they also increased their understanding of key concepts, such as random genetic variation.

Buckley, Gobert, and Horwitz (2006) conducted a study of *BioLogica,* a software system linking simulations to text in the domain of genetics. The researchers analyzed logs of students' interactions with the instructional system as they attempted to solve science process tasks. For example, one task asked the student to manipulate the model of a genome so that a trait appears to skip a generation. Successful performance on these tasks, as well as a systematic approach to the tasks, correlated with gains in conceptual understanding measured by pretests and posttests, suggesting that development of science process skills supported the gains in conceptual understanding.

Scientific Discourse

Although the committee found no evidence that the use of simulations develops students' scientific discourse or argumentation, a few studies focusing on the goal of conceptual understanding illuminate the relationship between discourse and conceptual understanding. For example, research on *BGuILE*, a simulation-based curriculum unit for high school biology, suggests that by supporting and scaffolding students' construction of scientific arguments, the unit helps students to develop deep and accurate understanding of scientific phenomena (Sandoval, 2003; Sandoval and Reiser, 2004).

In another study, Keller et al. (2006) showed that the *PhET Circuit Construction Kit* simulation, which models the behavior of electric circuits, can be an effective tool for engaging students in productive discourse. Undergraduate students who were shown the simulation during the lecture demonstrated a comparatively much higher and statistically significant gain in conceptual understanding after discussing the modeled phenomenon with their peers, compared with students who were shown a physical demonstration or who were provided with an equivalent verbal explanation to discuss with their peers.

Identity

The committee did not find any research evidence about whether the use of simulations may encourage students to think about themselves as science learners and develop an identity as someone who knows about, uses, and sometimes contributes to science.

EFFECTIVENESS OF GAMES

Evidence about the effectiveness of games in supporting science learning is only beginning to emerge, and the body of evidence is much smaller and weaker than the body of evidence related to the effectiveness of simulations. Most studies have not included control groups that would allow comparisons with other forms of science instruction. The limited evidence available, based on only a few examples, suggests that games can motivate interest in science and enhance conceptual understanding. Overall, however, the research remains inconclusive.

Motivation

Because one of the defining features of games is that they are fun, it is not surprising that researchers have studied the role of games in sparking interest in science and science learning. Several studies of *River City* suggest that it increases middle school students' motivation for science learning (this game-based curriculum unit is described in Chapter 1).

An early study compared two Boston area public middle school classes using the pilot version of *River City* with two matched control classes in which students received inquiry-oriented instruction focusing on the same science learning goals. The control instruction presented the same challenge as the game—to identify the causes of diseases in a historic American city—and engaged students in designing and conducting experiments—but did not include the game. There were 45 students in the two *River City* classes and 36 students in the control classes, split evenly by gender. About half of the ethnically diverse study participants were English language learners, and the majority qualified for free and reduced-price meals. All participants completed a pretest and posttest focusing on affective dimensions of science learning, including scales designed to measure motivation and perceived self-efficacy. On the motivation scales, the *River City* group, on average, gained more from pretest to posttest than the control group. On the perceived self-efficacy scales, the *River City* group's gains were significantly higher than the control group (Dede, Ketelhut, and Ruess, 2002).

Later, Ketelhut et al. (2006) compared middle school classrooms in which students were randomly assigned to one of three variations of *River City* with matched control classrooms in which students received similar instruction without the game, as described above. Approximately 2,000 ethnically diverse adolescents in eight public schools participated in the study, including large percentages of minorities, English language learners, and students eligible for free and reduced-price meals. All participants completed a pretest and posttest focusing on affective dimensions of science learning; one subscale measured interest in a scientific career. The *River City* group gained 5 percent more on this subscale than the control group. In addition, the authors found that in the *River City* classrooms, students and teachers were highly engaged, student attendance improved, and disruptive behavior dropped during the 3-week implementation period. In interviews, students who played *River City* reported that they were motivated by the ability to conduct inquiry, along with the ability to use virtual tools, such as bug catchers and microscopes to aid in their investigations (Ketelhut, 2007).

Tuzan (2004) found that students participating in *Quest Atlantis* (described later in this chapter) were motivated by a large number of game elements centered on identity, play, immersion, and social relationships. Barab, Arici, and Jackson (2005) found, based on their iterative design process in creating and modifying *Quest Atlantis*, that a strong narrative was one element supporting engagement.

Another study focused on the introduction of the Whypox disease in the virtual gaming community of *Whyville* (Neulight et al., 2007). Two classes with a total of 46 sixth-grade students, including an equal number of boys and girls, joined *Whyville* and played the game both at home and in science class. The students attended a laboratory school affiliated with a large urban university. They were ethnically diverse (27 percent Hispanic, 13 percent black, 13 percent Asian, and 47 percent white), and two-thirds received tuition assistance. Over 85 percent had computer and Internet access at home.

In this study, *Whyville* was integrated into a 10-week, teacher-led curriculum about infectious diseases that also included watching videos, examining cell structures under the microscope, doing experiments, and completing worksheets. *Whyville* was introduced in week 3, and the Whypox epidemic arrived in week 5. When a student's avatar contracted Whypox, its appearance changed, and the student's ability to chat declined. The researchers videotaped the classrooms and administered a survey about infectious disease before and after the curriculum unit.

Responding to the survey, the majority of study participants (61.5 percent) reported that they were motivated to learn more about the scientific phenomenon of the Whypox epidemic by the emotional impact of the disease. Those whose avatars were infected described the experience as "terrible," "annoying," and "frustrating," partly because sneezing interrupted their conversations with friends. Players increased their visits to the virtual Centers for Disease Control and Prevention to learn more about Whypox, where they could use two simulators to make and test predictions about the spread of the disease. In a further study, Kafai, Quintero, and Feldon (2010) found that, during Whypox outbreaks, simulation usage peaked with more than 1,400 simulations performed by 171 players. The authors found that 68 percent of the players conducted some form of systematic investigation by running the simulations three or more times.

Motivation Among Subpopulations

Like the disparities in science interest and achievement among young people of different genders, races, ethnicities, and socioeconomic status, there are also disparities in the engagement of different populations with video and computer games. A recent national survey of media use by children and youth aged 8 to 18 (Rideout, Foehr, and Roberts, 2010) indicates that, in 2009, boys spent an average of nearly an hour per day playing console video games and girls spent less than a quarter hour. Boys also spent more time with computers than girls, primarily because they spent an average of 25 minutes daily playing computer video games, whereas girls spent only 8 minutes per day playing such games. Black and Hispanic youth of both genders spent significantly more time playing video games than did white youth.

In light of these disparities, research on the role of games in sparking excitement and interest in science and science learning among diverse student groups is particularly important. To date, however, only a few investigators have examined this important issue. In the large study of *River City* described above, all students (regardless of gender, ethnicity, or English language proficiency) were more engaged in inquiry when playing *River City*, and preliminary data analysis suggests that they gained as much or more in content knowledge than the students in the control group (Ketelhut et al., 2007; Nelson, 2007).

Plass et al. (2009) conducted another study that addressed interest in science (computer science) among different groups of students. The researchers created a gaming environment, called *Peeps*, that was designed to engage girls in learning computer programming by inviting them to design parts of the game. In the game, students (both boys and girls) play a female character that interacts with the inhabitants of the virtual world by dancing with them. Students create dances by using increasingly complex computer programming skills, and they must also avoid a character designed to steal pieces of computer code that players have developed or acquired during the game.

The 59 study participants, sixth graders in an urban school in a large Northeastern city, included approximately equal numbers of ethnically diverse boys and girls. Participants played the game during four sessions over the course of one month, completed two missions designed to assess programming knowledge, and responded to surveys. The results suggested that playing the game increased feelings of general self-efficacy among female students and general self-esteem among both female and male students. Playing the game also appeared to increase self-efficacy in using computers among male, but not female, students. Finally, although the game did not appear to increase programming knowledge among students of either gender, it did appear to increase feelings of self-efficacy in the area of computer programming among both female and male students.

Some recent research suggests that gender differences in interest in games and responses to games may be diminishing (see Chapter 4).

Conceptual Understanding

Evidence about the role of games in conceptual understanding of science topics is only beginning to emerge and is inconclusive. Some examples are provided below.

Moreno and Mayer conducted a series of laboratory studies to investigate the impact of a computer game on students' retention of science content and their ability to transfer their knowledge to solve new types of problems. In two experiments (Moreno and Mayer, 2000), undergraduate student volunteers played a computer game about environmental science that included personalized (first- and second-person language) instructional content, delivered as narrated speech by a pedagogical agent.[1] Students who heard personalized content outperformed students who received neutral content on assessment questions focused on retention of science content as well as on questions focused on transfer of problem-solving skills. When Moreno and Mayer (2004) continued these studies and added a dimension that involved wearing a head-mounted display, they found that this display did not impact learning. In a follow-up study using the same game but with personalized content delivered via text (not voice), Moreno and Mayer (2007) found similar results. Students who saw personalized content outperformed students who received neutral content on questions designed to measure transfer of problem-solving skills and retention.

Another series of studies focused on the *Supercharged* game (Barnett et al., 2004; Jenkins, Squire, and Tan, 2004). In this three-dimensional game, players use the properties of charged particles and field lines to navigate their ship through space. Three middle school classes participated in a mixed methods pilot study comparing learning outcomes among students playing

---

[1]A pedagogical agent is an animated computer character that responds to stimuli, such as keyboard input or mouse clicks. It can be designed to support learning by posing questions, by evaluating the learner's level of understanding and responding appropriately, or by other methods.

Supercharged with outcomes among students using a guided inquiry curriculum. Average posttest scores were significantly higher for the students who played *Supercharged*. Anderson and Barnett (in press) continued the investigation of *Supercharged* with preservice elementary teachers. The control group in the study learned through a series of guided inquiry methods, and the experimental group played *Supercharged* during the lab sessions of the course. The students who played the game significantly outperformed the control students in terms of pre-post assessment gains.

In the study of *Whyville* discussed above, Neulight et al. (2007) investigated conceptual understanding of disease transmission among the sixth-grade students. Analyzing pretest and posttest results, the authors found a significant shift toward biologically correct explanations. By the end of the game-centered instructional unit, twice as many students applied biological reasoning when reasoning about natural infectious disease.

Clark et al. (2010) analyzed pre-post test data from 24 undergraduate and graduate students playing *SURGE*, a game focused on increasing students' understanding of specific relationships that are central to Newtonian mechanics. The data not only reinforce the potential of games to help students learn, but also underscore their potential to reinforce alternative conceptions. The game actually resulted in a significant decrease in scores on one posttest item by unintentionally focusing students' attention on another physics relationship that was not supported by the game. When this posttest item was excluded, the students demonstrated significant gains on the rest of the posttest. Data from interviews with the students indicate that players made successful (although variable) use of growing tacit understanding of the physics concepts involved to complete levels of the game.

There is some evidence that commercial games, not designed for science, can support conceptual understanding of science topics. For example, Holbert (2009) conducted ethnographic observations of and individual clinical interviews with children playing popular video games (*Mario Kart Wii* and *Burnout Paradise*). He found that children's intuitive thoughts about velocity, acceleration, and momentum were activated as they played these games. These intuitive ideas have been shown to play productive roles in the development of understanding of physics (diSessa, 1993; Roschelle, 1991).

Science Process Skills and Understanding of the Nature of Science

Research on two games designed for use in science classrooms—*Quest Atlantis* and *River City*—has examined development of science process skills.

In *Quest Atlantis*, players use an avatar to travel to virtual places and carry out quests, talk with other users and mentors, and develop their avatars. A quest is designed to be both entertaining and educational, as players participate in real-world and simulated activities focusing on the story of Atlantis—a complex civilization in need of help. The game includes a virtual world called Taiga Park and a story line in which the park experiences a decline in fish numbers, causing the fishing company, which generates revenue for the park, to threaten to leave. Three groups involved with the park—an indigenous population, a logging company, and a fishing company—disagree about the cause of the declining fish population. Working in small groups, students assist the park ranger by interviewing people with different perspectives on the problem, collecting and analyzing data to develop a hypothesis about the problem, and then proposing informed solutions (Barab et al., 2007).

Hickey, Ingram-Goble, and Jameson (2009) conducted a comparative study of the Taiga Park curriculum unit. A single sixth-grade teacher taught four science classes, using Taiga Park in two classes and a custom textbook addressing all of the same topics in the other two classes, over the course of 4 weeks. The teacher was in a school serving relatively high-achieving students in a Midwestern university town. Less than 20 percent of the schools' students qualified for free and reduced-price meals and about 90 percent were white. The authors measured content and inquiry skills using two types of assessments. The first consisted of open-ended performance assessment items that asked students to solve new water quality problems and provide a rationale for the solutions they proposed. The other was a pool of randomly sampled, released achievement test items that were aligned to targeted science content and inquiry standards but independent of the water quality focus of the Taiga curriculum. The authors compared pre-post scores on both types of assessments among the Taiga Park and control classes and found that the Taiga Park classes showed significantly larger gains in conceptual understanding and science process skills. Two new types of virtual formative feedback included in the game the following year resulted in substantially larger gains in both conceptual understanding and science processes as measured by the two assessments.

Several studies of River City have also investigated science process skills. In the large comparative study described above, Ketelhut et al. (2006) administered a pre- and post-affective assessment that included questions designed to measure thoughtfulness of inquiry. On these questions, the average gains of students using two of the three versions of River City were significantly higher than those of students in the control classrooms. The authors also measured learning outcomes using a pretest and posttest focusing on content and science process skills, and found no significant difference among the three experimental groups and the control group. In a further analysis, Ketelhut et al. (in press) looked for and scored evidence of inquiry in a random sample of 224 student "letters to the mayor," written at the end of their investigations by students in the experimental and control groups. Letters by students using a version of *River City* with additional guidance scored significantly higher in overall quality than letters by students in the control and other treatment groups. They were also significantly higher in specific dimensions of inquiry, such as stating a testable hypothesis, awareness that different symptoms were related to different diseases, and stating a conclusion.

Another study suggests that one form of *River City* may help students gain in understanding of the nature of science. Nelson (2007) explored the impact of embedded guidance messages in *River City*. The author found that increased viewing of guidance messages was associated with significantly higher score gains on assessment questions related to the nature of scientific inquiry and on questions about conceptual knowledge of disease transmission.

Perceptual and Spatial Abilities

Researchers are studying how games may influence perceptual and spatial abilities that play a role in development of science process skills. For example, experimental neuroscientists investigate how "action games"—that is, fast-paced, first-person shooter games in three-dimensional environments—may influence the ability to focus on a topic of interest while ignoring all other information. Green and Bavelier (2006) conducted a comparison study of action and nonaction gamers. The action gamers spent 10 hours playing an action game (*Medal of Honor, Unreal Tournament,* or *Call of Duty*), while the nonaction gamers played a control game (*Tetris* or *The Sims*) for 10 hours. The action gamers were better than the nonaction game players in two different types of performance tasks designed to measure visual attention.

Other studies focus on visual acuity. Li et al. (2009) compared the effects of training young people for 50 hours in either an action game (*Unreal Tournament 2004* or *Call of Duty*) or a nonaction game (*The Sims 2*). The action gamers experienced a marked improvement in contrast sensitivity. Calzato et al. (2010) found that, when action game players switched tasks, they lost less time than individuals that typically do not play such fast-paced, action-packed games. Finally, Dye, Green, and Bavelier (2009) found that action gamers were on average 12 percent faster than nonaction gamers at several visual tasks while being equally accurate.

Scientific Discourse

Few researchers have examined whether the use of games may affect students' scientific discourse or argumentation. In one study, Kafai (2009) analyzed chat data among *Whyville* players in an after-school setting following the onset of Whypox. Conversations about the disease rose dramatically and players engaged in "serious argumentation" about the epidemic. In another study of *Whyville*, Kafai, Quintero, and Feldon (2010) identified increases in students' use of type 2 vocabulary—that is, words, such as "contamination," that are not everyday words but are also not entirely scientific ("E. coli" is a scientific term). Type 2 vocabulary has been shown to be critically important for struggling readers' success in school (see Beck, McKeown, and Kucan, 2002).

Squire (2010) also reported increasing use of, and understanding of, type 2 scientific vocabulary among students playing an augmented reality game in science classrooms. The students used type 2 words in discussions, reports, and presentations as they played the role of scientists and gained proto-experiences of "authentic" scientific inquiry. Although this study reported findings about increased scientific discourse in classroom settings, such increases have also been identified among students playing augmented reality games in museums and after-school settings (Klopfer, 2008; Squire and Jan, 2007).

Barab et al. (2007), in the study of the Taiga Park curriculum unit in *Quest Atlantis* described above, found that the Taiga Park students were actively engaged in discourse related to the inquiry tasks of the curriculum and that they participated actively and productively in the inquiry practices of data gathering, negotiation, and data interpretation. Anderson (in press) found that embedded scaffolds in *Quest Atlantis* supported students in dialogue about the inquiry activities and in expressing as well as acquiring science content and process skills.

Steinkuehler and Duncan (2008) studied the discussion forums around the commercial, massively multiplayer, online role-playing game *World of Warcraft*, which focuses on fantasy themes. The authors' analysis of nearly 2,000 posts by users in 85 different discussion threads found that 86 percent of the posts involved social knowledge construction, more than 50 percent evidenced systems-based reasoning, roughly 10 percent evidenced model-based reasoning, and 65 percent displayed approaches to evaluating information that would support argumentation as a way to construct knowledge. Steinkuehler and Duncan argue that this is evidence that even popular commercial games without a direct connection to science can support discussions and thought processes that are similar to scientific discourse and reasoning.

Identity

Games have potential to help young people identify with science and science learning. Barab and Dede (2007, p. 1) propose, "Game-like virtual learning experiences can provide a strong sense of engagement and opportunities to learn for all students, even helping learners with low self-efficacy start afresh with a new 'identity' not tagged as an academic loser."

Many of the games described above engage students in playing the role of scientists, technicians, or others who need scientific knowledge to solve problems, and there is some evidence that this encourages them to identify with science. In interviews conducted as part of a *River City* study, students using the curriculum unit reported feeling like real scientists for the first time (Clarke and Dede, 2005). Researchers found significantly higher levels of "global science self-efficacy" among *River City* classes than among the matched control classes (Dede and Ketelhut, 2003), as well as significant gains in self-efficacy in scientific inquiry among *River City* classes (Dieterle, 2009).

Rosenbaum, Klopfer, and Perry (2006) studied 21 urban high school students playing *Outbreak @ The Institute*, an augmented reality game in which players take on the roles of doctors, technicians, and public health experts trying to contain a disease outbreak. Surveys, video, and interviews of the students showed that they perceived the game as authentic, felt embodied in the game, engaged in the inquiry, and understood the dynamic nature of the model in the game.

While this research suggests that some games have encouraged some students to identify with science, no evidence is available on whether these feelings of identity persist over time. Longitudinal studies are needed to address this question.

DESIGN FEATURES THAT INFLUENCE LEARNING

The research discussed above suggests that certain design features of games and simulations influence learning as students engage in inquiry and discourse and grapple with complex science concepts. These design features may be part of a simulation or game, or they may be part of the larger instructional context. The preliminary list below should not be considered definitive or complete. Because most simulations and games incorporate multiple features, it is difficult to disentangle the unique contribution of any single one (Wilson et al., 2009). Nevertheless, the committee offers these design features as a guide for continuing, design-based research on simulations and games. Design-based research is an ongoing process of developing, testing, and revising a simulation or game to enhance effectiveness.

Focus on Clear Learning Goals

In the committee's view, carefully targeting one or more learning goals is an important design feature for both simulations and games. Science learning, including learning through inquiry, is enhanced when instruction is targeted to clearly defined learning goals (National Research Council, 2005b). Clearly defining the learning goal or goals of a simulation or game is an essential first step before considering other design features. This is because design features that may enhance conceptual learning may not be the same as design features that aim to motivate learners to pursue careers in science (Ketelhut, 2009).

Researchers have established focusing on clearly-defined learning goals as a design principle to improve the effectiveness of simulations. For example, Clark and Mayer (2003) drew on empirical evidence to propose the coherence principle. This principle emphasizes that all elements of a simulation should be directly related to the learning goals, avoiding extraneous information that could distract the learner, disrupt the learning process, or seduce them into incorrect understandings. More recently, Linn et al. (2010) stated, based on a review of the research, that simulations should minimize irrelevant cognitive demand that could otherwise distract students from the primary learning goal. Plass et al. (2009, p. 48) state that there is enough research evidence to identify the following design principle for simulations: "The efficacy of a simulation depends on the degree to which it is in line with learning objectives."

The more limited research on games also suggests that it is important to focus on clear learning goals. For example, in the study of *SURGE* described above, Clark et al. (2010) found that the game caused a significant decrease in scores on one posttest item by unintentionally focusing students' attention on another physics relationship that was not an intended learning goal.

Clear learning goals are critical for the design of assessments to measure the effectiveness of a simulation or game (Quellmalz et al., 2009). The learning goal must be clearly established as a basis for evaluating the effectiveness of any game or simulation, and such evaluations support further research and continued improvement.

Provide External Scaffolding

To address the challenges involved in inquiry learning, research currently focuses on developing scaffolds, or cognitive tools, to support learning (de Jong, 2006). Learning scaffolds for simulations and games may be internal, including many of the other design features discussed below, or they may be external (see Box 2-1).

The research discussed in this chapter highlights the value of external scaffolding. Many of the examples provide evidence that simulations enhance conceptual understanding of science when they are scaffolded with other forms of instruction in larger curriculum units (e.g., *ThinkerTools, NIELS, Biologica*). Linn et al. (2010) recommend that designers embed simulations in supportive instruction as an important design principle to enhance effectiveness. This design principle is similar to de Jong's (2005) guided-discovery principle, which focuses on addressing students' documented difficulty in all aspects of inquiry learning, whether in the classroom or laboratory or in

BOX 2-1
Scaffolding Learning in Simulations and Games

Traditionally, scaffolding is a process by which adults or more able peers provide supportive structures to help learners perform mature behaviors before they are ready to do so on their own. Scaffolds can also be built into an activity itself, as in the example of training wheels on a bicycle. Once learners exhibit mature or independent behavior, the scaffolds are removed or faded. Taken more expansively, scaffolding can also be viewed as a progression of just-manageable challenges that enable learners to climb to greater understanding and skills. Thus, as they develop independence at one activity, a new, more challenging activity can lead to the next round of support.

New technologies create new opportunities for scaffolding, for example, with adaptive systems that provide just-in-time hints or change problem difficulty. Simulations and games can be designed to permit learners to pursue different progressions to the same outcomes, depending on various factors, including student interest, prior knowledge, and success so far. Scaffolding can be proactive and built into learners' first attempts at an activity, or it can be reactive in response to when they are faced with a challenge that they can solve with a hint, question, prompt, or interactive resource. Games demonstrate that providing challenges and scaffolds in an appropriate balance can keep motivation high. Ideally, they also help students develop important dispositions that include identifying with scientific activities and content to help reach important science learning goals.

Building effective scaffolding is a multifaceted process. First, experts in a subject identify suitable learning tasks or challenges that will guide the learner to grapple with the important ideas or skills in productive ways. Second, it is important to develop the resource framework that learners can use to help achieve the task, for example, through experimentation, explanation, peer networking, or reading. Scaffolding is therefore provided both in the selection of the important ideas or skills and in the related educational tasks and resources that best support the learning. Third, when developing a complex set of ideas or skills, the developer must consider the progression of learning over time. Fourth, the high interactivity of games and simulations provides opportunities for contingent feedback and system responsiveness. When learners encounter a challenge or question that is beyond their immediate capacity, scaffolding of various forms allows them to make progress (e.g., hints, guidance, or simply turning off options).

a simulation (Mayer, 2004). The guided-discovery principle (de Jong, 2005) states that inquiry learning is more effective when simulations or simulation-based curriculum units provide guidance, such as domain-specific explanations or direct advice on when to perform certain actions.

External scaffolding also appears to enhance learning through games. Neulight et al. (2007) found that study participants who experienced the simulated Whypox virus in a classroom setting, in which they also learned about infectious diseases through other forms of instruction, experienced gains in conceptual understanding and in identification with the scientific enterprise. Other study participants, who played the game at home, did not advance in these two dimensions of science learning. In another study, Mayer, Mautone, and Prothero (2002) found that providing pretraining in the *Profile Game* before playing it, by showing players pictures of possible geological features that would need to be identified through the game, led to significantly better performance on identifying those geological features in the game.

Representation

Research on how people react to, and learn from, different forms of visual stimuli has been under way for decades. Early studies compared pictorial with text representations (Plass et al., 2009). More recent studies of simulations and games have focused on how information is represented on a continuum from more detailed and realistic to more stylized or abstract. Some research suggests that more realistic representations can be more effective than abstract symbols.

For example, Plass et al (2009) report on two experiments, both involving 80 to 90 students aged 16 to 18 in a large public high school in rural Texas. Nearly 90 percent of the students were of Hispanic descent, 40 percent were female, and they had not previously studied the topic addressed by the simulation—the behavior of a gas when heated. For the first experiment, participants were randomly assigned to one of two forms of the simulation, one of which incorporated only abstract symbols (e.g., numbers), while the other also incorporated icons—small pictures of flames representing temperature and weights representing pressure. After completing a questionnaire about prior chemistry experience and pretests of chemistry knowledge and self-efficacy, participants worked with the simulation for approximately 20 minutes. They then completed posttests of comprehension and transfer knowledge. When the authors found no significant difference in learning outcomes between the two groups, they hypothesized that it was because the learning task placed a low cognitive load (demand on working memory) on the students. For the second experiment, the investigators increased the simulation's cognitive load by including a chart that displayed the effects of changing the temperature or pressure of the gas. Comparing test results, the authors found significant positive differences in comprehension and self-efficacy for the group using the simulations with icons. Further analysis indicated that the added icons were especially beneficial for students with low prior knowledge of chemistry.

Other research suggests that representations that are too realistic may impede learners' ability to transfer their understanding to another domain. Son and Goldstone (2009) conducted a series of three experiments focusing on the scientific principle of competitive specialization. First, they compared intuitive descriptions with concrete (i.e., realistic) representations and found that intuitive descriptions led to enhanced domain-specific learning but also deterred transfer. Second, they alleviated the limited transfer by combining intuitive descriptions with idealized graphical elements. In the third experiment, they found that idealized graphics were more effective for learning and transfer than concrete graphics, even when unintuitive descriptions were applied to them. They concluded that idealized graphics enhance learning and transfer when compared with highly realistic graphics. In addition, research on the two-dimensional, cartoonlike *Whyville* game discussed above suggests that a high degree of realism is not always necessary to support science learning. Based on their review of research on education and training with games, Wilson et al. (2009) propose that as the degree of realism of the task in a game increases, psychomotor skill learning will also increase but then level off.

Finally, representation is related to the learning goals of the simulation or game. Clear learning goals can help designers focus on the perceptual salience of the information displayed. For example, in a simulation about harmonic motion, Parnafes (2007) noted that students typically tended to attend to the perceptually salient features of the simulation rather than the conceptually important features (features an expert would attend to). This study suggests that, when designing simulations, it is important that the salient features of the simulation are ones that will be most productive in terms of the targeted learning goals.

Narrative/Fantasy

Narrative, sometimes called fantasy, is an extremely important feature of games. It engages learners, allows them to interact with the game without fear of real-life consequences, and makes them feel immersed in the game (Wilson et al., 2009). Without a strong narrative, a game designed for informal use may not attract players and a game designed for classroom use will not generate excitement, interest, or enthusiasm for science learning. Barab, Arici, and Jackson (2005) found, based on their iterative design process in creating and modifying *Quest Atlantis*, that a strong narrative was one element supporting engagement. In a further study of *Quest Atlantis*, Barab et al. (2007) observed that students saw an erosion diagram as part of the narrative, rather than an abstract representation of the scientific process of erosion. The authors suggest that too much narrative might hinder learning of formal scientific concepts, principles, and methods, making it difficult for students to distinguish these concepts from the particular situation in the game. Thus, game developers must carefully balance context with content.

The narrative in games designed for science learning often presents players with a question, problem, or mission that requires information to respond. Wilson et al. (2009) refer to this type of narrative as "mystery" and propose that learner motivation is positively related to the level of mystery in a game.

Feedback

An extensive body of research supports the view that providing learners with feedback enhances learning, and this also appears to be the case when using simulations and games. For example, the "reflection prompts" in *ThinkerTools* encouraged students to reflect on their own thinking, which in turn led to gains in both science process skills and conceptual understanding (White and Frederikson, 1998). Rieber, Tzeng, and Tribble (2004) found that students given graphical feedback during a simulation on laws of motion with short explanations far outperformed those given only textual information.

Moreno and Mayer (2000, 2004) conducted a series of studies to investigate the impact of design principles applied to computer games on student retention of science content and on problem-solving transfer questions. In one of these studies, undergraduate university students played a computer game about environmental science that included personalized instructional content, delivered as narrated speech by a pedagogical agent. Students who heard personalized content outperformed students who received neutral content. In another study, Moreno and Mayer (2005) compared using the pedagogical agent to give only corrective feedback (communicating to the learner whether she or he is right or wrong) with using it to give explanatory feedback (learners were told whether or not they were correct and were also given an explanation of why the answer was right or wrong). They found that providing explanatory feedback increased retention and transfer of the targeted concepts.

Nelson (2007) conducted a *River City* study in which he explored the impact of embedded guidance messages on student understanding of real-world science inquiry processes and knowledge. He found that increased viewing of guidance messages was associated with significantly higher score gains on a test focusing on knowledge of disease transmission.

User Control

Clark et al. (2009) identified the degree of user control as a dimension of simulations. However, the research reviewed above suggests that user control is an important feature of games as well. The optimal degree of user control in a given simulation or game is related to the science learning goal or goals targeted. For example, the limited degree of control provided to users of *PhET* simulations appears to be well aligned with the goals of these simulations—to increase conceptual understanding of specific science topics.

If the goal of a simulation or game is to increase science process skills and understanding, the research suggests that the degree of user control must be carefully balanced. On one hand, providing some autonomy to design and carry out virtual experiments appears to engage and motivate users of *River City* and *Quest Atlantis*. On the other hand, students often become confused when allowed to engage in open-ended inquiry—whether in a school science laboratory or in a virtual inquiry environment (Mayer, 2004; Moreno and Mayer, 2005). Providing students with guidance along with some control—such as the feedback from a pedagogical agent described above (Moreno and Mayer, 2005)—appears to enhance learning of science processes as well as science content.

Plass, Homer, and Hayward (2009), based on their review of the research, identify manipulation of content as a design principle for effective simulations, proposing that, "learning from visualizations is improved when learners are able to manipulate the content of a dynamic visualization compared to when they are not able to do so" (p. 49). Among other studies supporting this principle is a comparative study of two forms of a chemistry simulation—one that allowed the user to manipulate the content (e.g., the temperature and pressure of a gas) and one that allowed the user to only control pacing (Plass et al., 2007). Study participants who interacted with the simulation that allowed content manipulation demonstrated larger learning gains than those who were only allowed to control pacing.

Wilson et al.(2009), in their review of the research on gaming, report that allowing learners to navigate through a computer program based on their personal preferences leads to more positive attitudes and higher cognitive outcomes (Vogel et al., 2006). They also found that game players value control at all levels, from simply picking out a wardrobe or specific facial features for their avatars to determining strategies in game play. The authors propose that increasing the amount of control given to learners using games will positively affect skill-based learning.

Individual Learner Differences

The studies discussed above suggest that differences among individuals influence how they respond to, and learn from, simulations and games. For example, students with lower science achievement, as measured by a pretest, experienced greater gains in inquiry and content knowledge after using *ThinkerTools* (White and Frederiksen, 1998). Plass et al. (2009) found that adding icons that represented temperature and pressure concretely (as opposed to only abstract symbols) improved understanding of gas laws, especially among learners with low prior knowledge of the topic. These findings suggest that it is important to consider the target audience when designing a simulation or game and also to include adaptive features that modify the pace and type of information, based on user responses.

LIMITATIONS OF THE RESEARCH

The preceding discussion reveals many gaps and weaknesses in the body of research on the use of simulations and games for science learning. Although both simulations and games have been used for training and education for over three decades, they have not been studied systematically (Clark et al., 2009). Rapid changes in technology and delivery platforms result in changing definitions of what constitutes a game or a simulation, making it difficult to focus the research. Another problem is that researchers do not always describe the context for the interaction with the simulation or game, including other instructional support that might be provided in a classroom setting or informally by peers, making it difficult to separate out the unique contribution of the simulation or game. In addition, researchers sometimes fail to examine or report important variables related to student abilities and attitudes, such as previous science knowledge and previous experience with simulations or games. Another limitation is that studies have usually involved small groups of students with little diversity, making it difficult to generalize the results to the large, diverse population of U.S. science students.

The studies of games and simulations reviewed in this chapter unevenly address the methodological challenge associated with how to model outcomes that are by their very nature "nested" (students within classrooms or recitation sections, classrooms within schools or universities). The authors of several studies randomly assigned classrooms to different treatments (e.g., different versions of a simulation) or to treatment and control conditions, but analyzed and reported on data from individual students. These studies must be interpreted with caution, as the analysis of student-level data may lead to findings of statistically significant effects that are not warranted.[2]

---

[2]See Bryk and Raudenbush (1992) for a detailed treatment of this issue.

The questions researchers have asked about the effectiveness of simulations and games for learning, as well as the methods they have used, reflect a wide range of theoretical perspectives on how people learn. For example, the theoretical perspectives of neuroscientists studying how playing action video games affects visual response times are quite different from the theoretical perspectives underlying studies of how interactions with simulations affect understanding of science concepts. Reflecting these diverse perspectives, investigators have used a range of different research methods to measure the learning outcomes of simulations or games. The wide distribution of the published research evidence across journals in a variety of different disciplines makes it difficult to build on and extend a coherent base of research across studies and over time.

Another problem is that researchers studying games and simulations have not given enough attention to the adequacy of the instruments used to measure student outcomes (Quellmalz, Timms, and Schneider, 2009). Assessments are often designed to measure conceptual understanding alone, rather than other learning goals, and generally rely on paper and pencil tests, rather than taking advantage of digital technology to embed assessments in simulations or games (see Chapter 5). As a result, there is only limited evidence related to many of the five learning goals.

The research on games is particularly limited. Game designers often study potential users' reactions to and experience of a game to gauge consumer acceptance, but they rarely conduct formal research on science learning. Another challenge is that games are often designed for informal learning by self-selected users. Because of these challenges, only a few scholarly studies have been conducted. O'Neil, Wainess, and Baker (2005) searched three databases for studies of the effectiveness of games for learning and training published over a 15-year period and also conducted a hand search of journals for the year 2004-2005. Among the several thousand articles about games, the authors were able to identify only 19 articles that had been published in peer-reviewed journals and provided empirical information on the effectiveness of games. Although studies have documented the effectiveness of particular games to support learning among specific populations, it is unclear whether, or to what extent, the study findings can be generalized to other populations of learners (Hays, 2005).

All of these challenges make it difficult to build a coherent base of evidence that could demonstrate the effectiveness of simulations and games and inform future design improvements. Experts do not agree on the best directions for future research and development to support science learning. The field needs a process that will allow research evidence to accumulate across the variety of simulations and games and in the face of the constant innovation that characterizes them.

CONCLUSIONS

Science learning is a complex process involving multiple learning goals. A simulation or game can be designed to advance one or more science learning goals.

Conclusion: *Simulations and games have potential to advance multiple science learning goals, including motivation to learn science, conceptual understanding, science process skills, understanding of the nature of science, scientific discourse and argumentation, and identification with science and science learning.*

There is promising evidence that simulations enhance conceptual understanding, but effectiveness in conveying science concepts requires good design, testing, and proper scaffolding of the learning experience itself.

Conclusion: *Most studies of simulations have focused on conceptual understanding, providing promising evidence that simulations can advance this science learning goal. There is moderate evidence that simulations motivate students' interest in science and science learning. Less evidence is available about whether simulations support development of science process skills and other science learning goals.*

The emerging body of evidence about the effectiveness of games in supporting science learning is much smaller and weaker than the body of evidence about the effectiveness of simulations. Research on a few examples suggests that games can motivate interest in science and enhance conceptual understanding, but overall it is inconclusive.

Conclusion: *Evidence for the effectiveness of games for supporting science learning is emerging, but is currently inconclusive. To date, the research base is very limited.*

The available research suggests that differences among individual learners influence how they respond to, and learn from, simulations and games. Some studies of simulations have found that students with lower prior knowledge experienced greater gains in targeted learning goals than students with more prior knowledge related to these goals. Differences across gender and race in young people's use of commercial games could potentially influence their motivation to use games for science learning; however, a few studies of games have demonstrated gains in science learning across students of different genders, races, English language ability, and socioeconomic status.

Conclusion: *Emerging evidence indicates that different individuals and groups of learners respond differently to features of games and simulations.*

Although the research evidence related to science learning through interaction with simulations is stronger and deeper than that related to games, the overall research base is thin. Development of simulations and games has outpaced research and development of assessment of their learning outcomes, limiting the amount of evidence related to other learning goals beyond conceptual understanding.

Conclusion: *The many gaps and weaknesses in the body of research on the use of simulations and games for science learning make it difficult to build a coherent base of evidence that could demonstrate their effectiveness and inform future improvements. The field needs a process that will allow research evidence to accumulate across the variety of simulations and games and in the face of the constant innovation that characterizes them.*

3

Simulations and Games in the Classroom

This chapter considers the use of simulations and games for science learning in the context of formal education. After describing the variety of contexts in which individuals interact with simulations and games, it discusses opportunities for using simulations and games in classrooms as well as constraints on their use. It goes on to outline alternative approaches to addressing these constraints and realizing the potential of simulations and games to support learning in science classrooms. The chapter ends with conclusions and recommendations.

INTRODUCTION: LEARNING CONTEXTS

Individuals interact with simulations and games in a variety of different contexts, comprised of interrelated physical, social, cultural, and technological dimensions (Ito, 2009; National Research Council, 2009). One dimension is the physical setting, either the formal environment of a school or university science classroom or an informal learning environment (the home, museum, after-school program, or other setting). Dimensions of the context that may influence learning include the involvement of other participants, who they are (experts, peers, family, teachers), and the technology itself (e.g., handheld devices, immersive environments provided on laptops).

Games and simulations can create local contexts that can similarly engage learners, whether at home, in school, or in after-school programs. At the same time, however, research has shown that the surrounding context can significantly shape how a learner interacts with a simulation or game and the extent to which this interaction supports science learning (Linn et al., 2010). Perhaps the most important psychological difference between using a simulation or game at school or college and using it informally is motivation. In the context of formal education, the professor or teacher requires the students to interact with the simulation or game, and the students may or may not be motivated. In informal contexts, individuals play a game or manipulate a simulation for fun, motivated by their own interest and enjoyment (see Chapter 4 for further discussion). Reflecting this difference, most studies have focused on using educational simulations and games in either a formal or informal context; few have explored their potential to support learning across the boundaries of time and place. This chapter therefore focuses on formal educational settings, and informal settings are discussed separately in the following chapter.

OPPORTUNITIES

Simulations and games have great potential to improve science learning in elementary, secondary, and undergraduate science classrooms. They can individualize learning to match the pace, interests, and capabilities of each particular student and contextualize learning in engaging virtual environments. Because schools serve all students, increased use of simulations and games in science classrooms could potentially improve access to high-quality learning experiences for diverse urban, suburban, and rural students. The U.S. Department of Education's (2010) draft National Education Technology Plan states (p. vi):

> The challenge for our education system is to leverage the learning sciences and modern technology to create engaging, relevant, and personalized learning experiences for all learners that mirror students' daily lives and the reality of their futures.

In higher education, where faculty members generally have more control over selection of curriculum and teaching methods than do K-12 teachers, the use of simulations is growing. The number of higher education institutions accessing the *PhET* simulations online more than doubled over the past five years, from 580 in 2005-2006 to 1,297 in 2009-2010, and the number of online sessions by users at these institutions grew from 13,180 to 269,177[1] (Perkins, 2010). Among physics faculty responding to a 2008 survey about research-based instructional strategies, small proportions reported currently using other simulations and simulation-based learning environments, including *Physlets* (13.0 percent), *RealTime* physics virtual laboratories (7.3 percent), and *Open Source Physics* (21.8 percent) (Henderson and Dancy, 2009).

The use of simulations and virtual laboratory packages is also gaining

---

[1]The *PhET* simulations can also be downloaded and installed for use offline, but no data are available on the number of offline sessions.

momentum in high schools and middle schools (Scalise et al., 2009), and games are being tested in a few schools and districts. In K-12 settings, science teachers may use a simulation or game to engage students' interest at the beginning of a unit of instruction, build understanding of a particular topic in the unit, or as a form of assessment. Alternatively, a teacher, often in collaboration with researchers, may focus an extended unit of instruction on a simulation-based learning environment or game.

Opportunities in School Settings

Although many different types of simulations and games have been tested in K-12 and undergraduate classrooms, only a few have been widely implemented. Some examples are the Taiga Park curriculum unit in *Quest Atlantis*, which has been used by thousands of students in elementary schools, after-school clubs, and science centers, and the simulation-based learning environments developed by Songer, Kelcey, and Gotwals (2009), which have been used by hundreds of students in the Detroit Public Schools. The developers of the *River City* game-based curriculum unit have investigated the process of widely implementing the unit, as well as its effectiveness for learning (see Box 3-1). To capture lessons learned from this experience and research, the committee asked lead developer Christopher Dede (2009c) to outline the opportunities and constraints that formal classroom settings offer for simulations and games.

Dede (2009c) identified five opportunities that classroom settings offer for using simulations and games. First, the teacher is a resource to support learning and can also provide valuable information to developers on student misconceptions inadvertently generated by a game or simulation. For example, a teacher observed that a student team using *River City* once spent substantial time repeatedly using the mosquito catcher (a virtual tool to help students assess the local prevalence of insects that serve as a vector for malaria), well beyond what was needed for statistical sampling. When she investigated, she found that the students believed they could reduce illness in the simulation by "catching" enough mosquitoes to block the disease. The teacher informed the developers, who used this feedback to modify the instructions for playing the game.

Second, classroom settings offer the opportunity to reach students who might otherwise view science as boring. The growing popularity of gaming outside school reduces teachers' work to prepare students for using educational simulations and games and builds learners' motivation for them. Some students who enjoy gaming for entertainment but shun educational games find that assigned gaming experiences in the classroom are unexpectedly fascinating, building their interest and self-efficacy in school (Clarke, 2006; Ketelhut, 2007).

Third, the responsibility of the teacher to grade students can present

---

BOX 3-1
Implementation of *River City*

In 2002, *River City* was piloted, along with a matched control curriculum, in three Boston area public schools with large percentages of English language learners and students eligible for free and reduced-price meals. A total of 63 sixth- and seventh-grade students participated in the *River City* unit, and an additional 36 students received the control curriculum. The students used either *River City* or the control curriculum during their regularly scheduled science classes over the course of two weeks. In 2003-2004, three variations of the curriculum unit, along with the matched control curriculum, were tested in urban schools in New England, the Midwest, California, and the Southeast (Ketelhut et al., 2006). Like the students involved in the pilot, the 2,500 urban students in this larger test included large percentages of English language learners and students eligible for free and reduced-price meals. By 2007, over 8,000 students had been taught using *River City* (Ketelhut, 2007).

---

both an opportunity and a constraint. Students and teachers using *River City* reported that, when the learning experience was evaluated by the teacher as part of the course grade, some students took the game or simulation more seriously, while others lost engagement. Fourth, classrooms present the opportunity to use study designs that control for confounding variables, allowing researchers to more clearly isolate whether, and to what extent, a simulation or game affects student learning. Finally, public schools offer the opportunity to deliver educational games and simulations to an entire population of students, scaling up the potential learning gains.

Opportunities for Individualized Learning

Simulations and games designed for science learning allow the learner some control over the pacing and content of the learning. This and other features provide the possibility of individualizing learning to match each learner's unique needs, strengths, and weaknesses. Classroom settings provide opportunities to both tap and extend this capacity (Dede, 2009b).

First, teachers can assign students to teams based on their knowledge of students' intellectual and psychosocial characteristics. For example, *River City* and other immersive learning environments use "jigsaw" pedagogies, in which each team member has access to data that others do not, requiring collaboration for collective success (Dede, 2009a). Teachers assigning students to these teams have worked to ensure that each team includes students with interests in science, in games, and in collaborative leadership. Teachers have also tried to place each learner in a role that matches his or her current capabilities. For example, students who struggle to read English text can aid their teams by gathering numeric data. Finally, teachers have tried to select team members so that one person does not dominate the interaction. Such nuanced composition of learning groups is much more difficult in unsupervised informal settings.

Second, science teachers can alter their classroom instruction and support on the basis of the feedback that games and simulations provide. For example, teachers working with the *River City* curriculum unit received daily, detailed logs of students' chats and behaviors, as well as their scores on embedded assessments and their postings in online notepads. Most teachers reported that they liked receiving these data (Dieterle et al., 2008). In classroom settings, the teacher can take advantage of feedback from the simulation or game to enhance and individualize learning—an opportunity that is not available in informal settings.

Third, science games and simulations can be adapted for students with special needs, allowing them to be mainstreamed in science classrooms. For example, the developers of an augmented reality curriculum adapted it to meet the needs of a student who was visually impaired (Dunleavy, Dede, and Mitchell, 2009). Hansen, Zapata-Rivera, and Feng (2009) are testing a new simulation-based learning system with integrated assessment that shows promise of supporting science learning for all students, including those with disabilities. As another illustration, a special needs teacher modified the *River City* curriculum so that her class of cognitively challenged students could complete a substantial part of the curriculum, with very positive effects on their motivation and self-efficacy. Classrooms offer opportunities for teachers to extend the supports that can be embedded in science games and simulations to meet special needs.

Fourth, educational games and simulations can potentially help prepare students to take full advantage of other science learning activities. For example, Metcalf, Clarke, and Dede (2009) are currently designing and studying a learning environment focusing on virtual ecosystems. The researchers plan to study whether students who experience this learning environment are better prepared to take full advantage of their visits to real ecosystems.

Fifth, teachers, through their knowledge of students, can relate virtual experiences in science games and simulations to what is happening in the real world or in students' lives. For example, some students in urban settings noted that the tenement houses in *River City* were infested by diseases that, over a century later, are still prevalent in their neighborhoods; immigrant students experiencing *River City* made similar observations about current conditions in their native countries. Teachers were instrumental in helping learners make these types of connections.

Further research is needed on what types of professional development are most effective in helping teachers to realize these opportunities for individualizing learning with simulations and games (Schwarz, Meyer, and Sharma, 2007).

Opportunities for Psychosocial Learning and Motivation

Games and simulations draw on psychosocial factors to motive and to educate. There is evidence that well-designed games and simulations can enhance students' psychosocial development, particularly in adolescence (Durkin, 2006), and schools can support this potential.

Schools provide a setting in which students can informally discuss simulations and games, complementing the more structured, formal discussions in their science classes. As described in the previous chapter, Steinkuehler and Duncan (2008) found evidence that online discussions of the commercial game *World of Warcraft* supported shared learning. In schools, teachers can leverage students' physical proximity to foster similar discussion and learning, face to face. For example, some *River City* teachers were amazed by students' eagerness to spend extra time on the curriculum during lunch hour or before or after school. By providing supervised access to the curriculum at these times, the schools allowed students to develop communication skills and social relationships centered on science learning.

Schools also host clubs and other organizations that provide opportunities for learning informally with simulations or games. The growth of robotics illustrates this potential; similar to augmented reality games, robotics adds a kinesthetic dimension to learning (Rogers and Portsmore, 2004). Science games and simulations may motivate informal learning in similar ways, if they allow the user to modify the game or simulation, similar to modifying one's robot. "Modding" is now possible in many games and is extensively used by many participants for fun and informal learning about the models underlying the entertainment experience. Some games (e.g., *Little Big Planet, Spore*) even require learner design of processes that involve scientific principles, although no support is provided for this. Science teachers can employ modding to encourage students to learn by designing simulations or games (Annetta et al., 2009; see Chapter 4 for further discussion).

CONSTRAINTS OF SCHOOL SETTINGS

Dede (2009c) identified several constraints on the use of educational games and simulations in formal classroom settings, some of which are closely related to the opportunities described above. One is that the classroom teacher may not always implement the game or simulation in the manner intended by its designers, inadvertently undercutting student learning. For example, although *River City* is designed to motivate and support students in moving from exploring the virtual environment to formulating and testing a hypothesis, some teachers have asked students to use the curriculum to simply confirm correct answers that the teachers provided in advance (Ketelhut et al., 2007). As noted in Chapter 1, students often find inquiry learning difficult (National Research Council, 2005b). To effectively help students through these difficulties, teachers require deep content knowledge and effective teaching strategies. These requirements, together with practical constraints, such as lack of time and the press of high-stakes science assessments focusing on content knowledge, may discourage teachers from using games to engage students in inquiry learning.

Another constraint is that schools often lack the technology infrastructure required to support a game or simulation. A chronic problem in implementing the *River City* curriculum has been teachers' lack of access to an adequate, reliable technology infrastructure. These problems include difficulty providing one-to-one student access to computers and challenges in obtaining network access to outside resources.

The requirement that teachers grade student work, including work with simulations and games, can also pose a constraint. Both students and teachers who worked with *River City* reported that, when the teacher evaluated students' learning in the curriculum as part of the course grade, some students became less engaged and interested, while others took the game more seriously. Another constraint is posed by current assessment methods. Current high-stakes science tests do not accurately measure the complex understandings and skills developed by high-quality simulations and games (Quellmalz et al., 2009), yet current education policy focuses on student performance on these high-stakes tests. This can discourage the use of simulations and games. For example, science curriculum coordinators for three large urban districts refused to allow teachers to use *River City* because an emphasis on science inquiry might interfere with students doing well on content-oriented high-stakes science tests (Clarke and Dede, 2009).

Although science classrooms offer opportunities for research designs that control some variables, obtaining permission to do research in schools is typically very difficult. For example, in taking the *River City* curriculum to scale, the developers had to satisfy one school district that demanded three times the documentation that the Harvard University institutional review board (IRB) required, mandated customized changes to the researchers' standard letters of consent approved by the Harvard IRB, and took almost a year to reach a favorable decision. Another district required researchers to be fingerprinted by the district, because the state refused to accept fingerprints done elsewhere. Other challenges arose in school districts due to breakdowns in internal communications between the curriculum, research, and technical departments.

ALTERNATIVE APPROACHES TO EXPANDING CLASSROOM USE

Experts have proposed alternative approaches to overcome these constraints and realize the opportunities for using simulations and games in classroom settings. For example, to address the constraint that teachers sometimes undercut the intended goals of a simulation or game, Dede (2009c) emphasized the value of teacher learning, both formal and informal. Teacher learning improves the fidelity of implementation of the curriculum. Among teachers using *River City*, the number of years of experience implementing the curriculum was significantly correlated with both greater teacher comfort with it and better learning outcomes for students. In addition, a large majority (94 percent) of teachers rated the developers' 4-hour online pre-implementation training as useful. Trainers working in the field to support *River City* reported fewer problems with teachers who participated in the developers' professional development. Students of teachers who were trained online performed significantly better on the posttest, on average (controlling for gender, socioeconomic status, reading level, and pretest performance), than students whose teachers were trained face to face. These findings on successful online training build on other research demonstrating the effectiveness of several models of online professional development (Dede, 2006; Falk and Drayton, 2009). Such research could lead to the emergence of new models of online professional development to help teachers adapt science games and simulations for effective use in their particular situations (Dede, 2009b).

To address technology constraints, the *River City* team included a part-time technology specialist to handle the unique school-by-school and district-by-district network configurations.[2] When technical problems arose, science teachers reported that often their students were adept at resolving them.

Horwitz (2009) suggests that both technology and assessment constraints could be addressed by outsourcing technology services to an educational service provider. The service provider would provide updated hardware and

---

[2]Schools systems and developers are exploring web-based delivery of games and simulations to avoid the need to install games on school networks (see Chapter 6).

software to support continued innovation in simulations and games and would maintain data on students' progress, as measured by embedded performance assessments, in secure databases. More broadly, financially self-sustaining educational service providers could provide simulations, games, and related curriculum, instruction, and assessment scaffolds to schools on an ongoing basis. These entities could potentially address the problem that technological innovations rarely last beyond the time frame of the grant-funded project that created them.[3] However, the logistics and business models of this approach have not yet matured.

Despite these possibilities to overcome constraints, Dede (2009c, p. 11) concluded that "current educational systems pose formidable challenges to implementation at scale." Noting that many variables influence adoption (or avoidance) of any educational intervention, he observed that scaling up an intervention is very difficult, even if it has been demonstrated as effective, economical, and logistically practical in a few classrooms (Dede, Honan, and Peters, 2005; Venkatesh and Bala, 2008).

One important variable influencing adoption is the learning goal (or goals) of the game or simulation. A simulation focusing on development of content knowledge—which is a widely accepted goal in current science education—may be less challenging, but also less transformative, for a teacher to use than a game that engages students in authentic scientific inquiry in a complex virtual environment (Dede, 2009b). The challenges of inquiry teaching and learning were noted earlier in this chapter. At the same time, state science standards and assessments emphasizing science facts encourage teachers to emphasize content knowledge, leaving little time for inquiry. Science teachers who use a game to engage students in inquiry will require extensive support to transform their teaching practices in the face of these challenges.

An Evolutionary Approach

In a response to Dede, Culp (2009) suggests that wider use of simulations and games to enhance learning might best be realized through incremental, evolutionary change, rather than dramatic shifts in teaching and learning approaches. Drawing on three decades of research on the integration of technology into classrooms, Culp (2009) argues that adoption of any educational intervention is driven not only by the factors discussed above—the personal capacity of teachers and the institutional capacity of schools and

---

[3]In a few cases, private foundations have solicited proposals from learning technology projects that are nearing the end of their federal grants. Foundations have selected the most promising proposals and provided funding to prepare the technologies for large-scale deployment and also to create a business plan.

districts—but also by other important realities. These realities, Culp argues, are often ignored when developers create electronic games for research purposes or to demonstrate proof of concept models. One of these realities is teachers' and administrators' view of the alignment between their local learning goals and priorities and the perceived goals of the proposed intervention. Another is teachers' perceptions of the extent of alignment between their students' existing, persistent learning needs and the perceived goals and effectiveness of the proposed intervention.

Culp (2009) pointed to technological tools that have been widely adopted in schools, including graphing calculators, probes linked to computers, and electronic whiteboards (Roschelle, Patton, and Tatar, 2007). Each of these tools is a discrete, freestanding piece of technology designed to address specific challenges or sticking points in learning that teachers are very familiar with. In addition, each is flexible and adaptable to many different curricular contexts and can be used simply at first and with growing sophistication over time.

Based on this analysis, Culp (2009) proposes using the design process to support incremental adoption of simulations and games. Specifically, she advocates designing simulations and games to be discrete, flexible, and adaptable by teachers and including expert teacher perspectives in the design process. In addition, she proposes mobilizing time and support for teachers to explore connections between specific electronic games or simulations and their own unique curriculum and teaching goals.

An Integrative Approach

Songer (2009) expressed another perspective, based on 15 years of experience in developing and testing simulation-based learning environments in Detroit Public Schools. She proposes that integration of technology into schools is critical to transform current science education. In her view, neither using technology to supplement the current curriculum nor conducting comparative studies of using technology versus no technology will dramatically improve students' science learning. Instead, she suggests integrating simulations and games into science instruction by following design principles that are, for the most part, identical to the basic design principles for supporting deep science learning more generally. These general design principles include focusing on a few big ideas in science (Linn et al., 2000); providing learners with systematic guidance to develop more complex ideas, including scaffolds for both content learning and inquiry reasoning; and allowing learners to systematically revisit and deepen their understandings.

Songer's research team has applied these general principles to development of digital learning environments built on publicly available scientific databases that are revised to be educationally focused and accessible to middle school learners. For example, the *Animal Diversity Web* designed for adult use has been revised to create an interactive *Critter Catalogue* that has been shown to support science process skills and understanding, questioning, and development of scientific explanations by fourth through sixth graders[4] (Songer, Kelcey, and Gotwals, 2009). Students using these environments have demonstrated growth in content understanding as well as complex reasoning.

In addition to the general design principles, Songer identified three instructional design principles that she sees as unique to technology-based learning: (1) engage learners in data gathering, modeling, and sharing; (2) support social construction of knowledge among learners; and (3) engage learners in role playing (in her research, students become authorities on the revised data sets). Songer concluded that simulations are essential to support students in thinking deeply about core science topics.

CONCLUSIONS

Individuals interact with simulations and games in a variety of different contexts, comprised of interrelated physical, social, cultural, and technological dimensions. These contexts influence the extent of interaction with simulations and games and whether, and to what extent, these interactions support learning.

Conclusion: *The context in which a simulation or game is used can significantly shape whether and how participants learn science.*

Simulations and games have great potential to improve science learning in K-12 and undergraduate science classrooms. They can individualize learning to match the pace, interests, and capabilities of each particular student and contextualize learning in engaging virtual environments. Because schools serve all students, increased use of simulations and games in science classrooms could potentially improve access to high-quality learning experiences for diverse urban, suburban, and rural students.

Conclusion: *Schools offer unique opportunities to embed a game or simulation in a supportive learning environment, to improve equity of access to high-quality learning activities, to individualize learning, and to increase the use of games for science learning.*

In K-12 education, inadequate infrastructure, institutional and organizational constraints, and lack of teacher and administrator understanding and

---

[4]This learning environment does not include simulations.

preparation pose challenges for using games and simulations to support learning. Simulations have been taken up more in higher education than in elementary or secondary education.

There are different models of implementing games and simulations in schools. In an evolutionary model, they can be designed to increase the productivity of learning without dramatic changes to current science teaching approaches. In other models, they can be designed to more dramatically transform science teaching and learning, advancing science process skills as well as conceptual understanding. The more transformative models require greater support for schools and teachers, and they may infuse technology into the whole instructional environment.

Conclusion: *There are currently many obstacles to embedding games and simulations in formal learning environments. However, alternative models for incorporating games and simulations in classrooms are beginning to emerge.*

Science educational standards that include many topics at each grade level pose a constraint to increased use of simulations and games in K-12 science classrooms. Simulations and games are often designed to support learners in thinking deeply about selected science concepts by engaging them in active investigations, but teachers and administrators may avoid using them because of the pressure to cover all of the topics included in current standards within limited time frames.

Conclusion: *Well-designed and widely accepted science standards, focusing on a few core ideas in science, could help to reduce the barriers to wider use of simulations and games posed by current state science standards. Such standards might potentially encourage the use of simulations and games.*

4

Simulations and Games in Informal Learning Contexts

This chapter begins by defining the informal contexts in which individuals interact with simulations and games. The second section discusses opportunities for learning with simulations and games that are offered by informal contexts, and the third section describes constraints that limit the use of simulations and games in these contexts. The fourth section focuses on approaches to overcoming these constraints, so that simulations and games can serve as a bridge, linking science learning across and between informal and formal contexts. The chapter ends with conclusions.

INFORMAL LEARNING CONTEXTS

Science learning in informal contexts differs from learning in formal contexts, such as classrooms or laboratories, in many respects (National Research Council, 2009). Squire and Patterson (2009) compared some of the key differences related to the use of games for learning in the two different contexts (see Table 4-1). The authors caution that comparing these differences along particular dimensions (such as how time is structured) is not intended to put informal contexts "in response" to formal contexts; informal contexts may be as important as formal settings in people's attitudes toward and experience of science (Barron, 2006; Crowley and Jacobs, 2002; National Research Council, 2009). They also note that formal educational contexts may vary considerably. Nevertheless, in general, informal science educators have more freedom than formal science educators in the science learning goals they pursue, how they pursue them, and the extent to which they need to appeal to audiences that can choose how to spend their time.

Informal contexts for science learning with simulations and games are diverse, varying along a number of dimensions, including the physical setting

TABLE 4-1 Comparison of Informal and Formal Contexts for Learning with Games

	Informal Contexts	Formal Contexts
Time Structure	Flexible	Rigid
Participation	Voluntary	Compulsory
Educational Goals	Emergent	Largely defined
Age Grouping	Flexible	Largely age divided
Degree of Authenticity	Potentially high	Generally low
Uniformity of Outcomes	Little	High
Disciplinary Boundaries	Flexible	Fixed

SOURCE: Squire and Patterson (2009). Reprinted with permission.

(e.g., a home, a school classroom hosting an after-school club, the outdoors), the social and cultural influences, and the technology supporting the simulation or game. Another dimension is the degree to which an individual's interaction with a simulation or game is structured, ranging from completely unstructured game-playing at home to highly structured workshops (Squire and Patterson, 2009).

OPPORTUNITIES PROVIDED BY INFORMAL SETTINGS

Squire and Patterson (2009) observe that informal science educators are largely free to pursue a variety of science learning goals, from increasing ethnic diversity among scientists, to increasing interest in science careers, to increasing the scientific literacy of the general population. This diversity in goals, together with the diversity of informal learning contexts, presents both an opportunity and a challenge. The opportunity is that educational game designers are free to create experiences that appeal to individual students' interests or span home, school, and after-school contexts. At the same time, however, this diversity of goals, contexts, and methods for reaching those goals makes for a fragmented field.

Freedom to Pursue Diverse Learning Goals

As an example of the opportunities for games in informal settings, DeVane, Durga, and Squire (2009) describe their attempts to build systemic ecological-economic thinking among *Civilization* game players in an after-school gaming club.[1] This curriculum linked ecological, economic, and

---

[1] *Civilization* is a historical simulation game. Players lead a civilization over a time period, managing its utilization of natural resources, cities' production, and strategic goals.

political concerns around a gaming series based on global sustainability (Brown, 1992). Such a curriculum might have been difficult to implement in schools that teach biology but not ecology, or that do not link either biology or ecology to economics and political science. DeVane, Durga, and Squire (2009) adapted *Civilization* to connect these topics, addressing food shortages, agricultural policy, trade relations, and environmental concerns. They reported that participants developed a type of systemic thinking about these topics across geopolitical systems (see Squire and Durga, in press). Pursuing this kind of broad educational goal may be much more feasible in informal settings than in classrooms focusing on individual academic disciplines.

As a voluntary after-school option, participants chose to take part in the gaming club over playing basketball, cooking, or scouting. Reflecting its voluntary nature, many students resisted taking pretests or posttests, making assessment difficult. As a result of this voluntary nature, informal educators are much more concerned with building and sustaining student interest than most formal educators (National Research Council, 2009). In fact, informal science educators have the unique opportunity to pursue goals that would be difficult to achieve in formalized settings.

Individualized Learning

When used in informal settings, games and simulations offer students opportunities to develop highly individualized interests and pursuits. Researchers have found that many students who participate in informal educational programs using information technology develop deep interest and expertise in areas ranging from computer programming to historical modeling (Bruckman, Jensen, and DeBonte, 2002; Resnick, Rusk, and Cooke, 1998; Squire, 2008a, 2008b). Such students develop learning communities that—like games culture in general—are built on a valuing of expertise (Squire, 2008b). In these learning communities, one's background or formal educational credentials are less important than one's ability to meet (and at times push the boundaries of) community norms. To illustrate this potential to individualize learning, Figure 4-1 depicts the trajectory of game players as they move from being competent players to becoming expert designers in *Apolyton University*. *Apolyton University* is an online informal learning environment that uses the narrative of a university and offers *Civilization* players various courses leading to credentials ("master's degrees" in the story line). Players participating in courses that require extended game-playing (upward of 100 hours) develop personalized and idiosyncratic skills that arise from an intersection among their interests, the affordances of the game, and the pathways made available in the game-playing community (Bruckman, Jensen, and DeBonte, 2002; DeVane, Durga, and Squire, 2009; Resnick, Rusk, and Cooke, 1998).

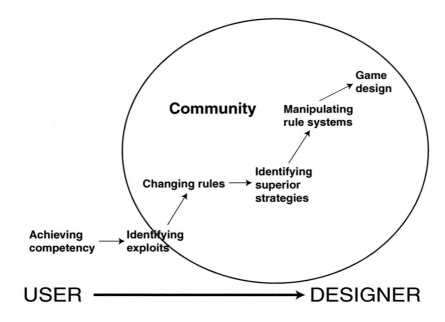

FIGURE 4-1 *Learning trajectories from user to designer among gamers.*
SOURCE: Squire and Patterson (2009). Reprinted with permission.

Generating Interest

The opportunity games provide to support individualized learning cannot be realized without grappling with the related opportunity and challenge of building and sustaining the learner's interest. Informal learning environments—like games themselves—ultimately are fueled by interest- or passion-driven learning. Like informal science educators generally, designers of games for learning have the task of designing enticing learning experiences that compel learners to learn more. For example, Klopfer (2008) described scientific mystery games at museums in which pairs of parents and students paid money to attend game-based learning workshops during their free time. Because individual learning is driven by individual interests, Squire and Patterson (2009) propose that the development of student interests and identities is a primary goal for informal science educators.

Event-Driven Learning

Games provide an opportunity for players to learn through virtual experiences, including particular virtual events. Kafai et al. (in press) show how the shared experience of the Whypox outbreak in *Whyville* provided a basis for shared community membership, engagement, and learning. Although other informal science learning activities, such as robotics or computer programming competitions, are also event driven, Whypox was unique in mobilizing hundreds of youth in authentic inquiry in real time to identify the cause and to minimize the impact of a disease that was personally meaningful to them. Educators might want to further develop the potential of this kind of event-driven learning. The multiple forms of participation enabled by informal learning communities around games could advance various learning goals, ranging from the development of deep expertise through long-term sustained participation to simply raising interest through short-term experiences.

Distributed Mentorship

In classrooms, the teacher may serve as a mentor and guide to support student learning. Educational games provide opportunities to distribute mentoring roles more widely to other adults, peers, or family members—in both formal and informal learning contexts. For example, Nulty and Shaffer (2008) found, in a study of fourth- and fifth-grade students who played *Digital Zoo* in a school classroom, that adults other than the teacher mentored students and enhanced their learning. The game engaged students in designing digital characters for an animated film. Students worked in teams with adult "design advisers," and the game concluded with each team of players presenting their design recommendations to other adults, who played the role of clients. Pre- and post-interviews with each player focused on the set of skills, knowledge, identity, values, and epistemology that engineers develop in their professional training. Players who reported that the adult mentors (design advisers and clients) helped them to think about their designs or themselves and their job differently were significantly more likely to demonstrate an increased understanding of the engineering frame. The authors concluded that adult mentors played a key role in helping the players understand engineering. Similarly, Kafai et al. (in press) noted the importance of mentors in their study of Whypox.

Opportunities for distributed mentorship are especially great when games are played in informal contexts. Researchers studying informal gaming have noted the development of learning communities and the importance of mentorship in these communities (Kafai et al., in press; Klopfer, 2008; Squire, 2008b; Squire and Patterson, 2009). As noted above, learners in these communities value expertise more than players' background or formal educational credentials. Games designed for science learning could potentially distribute teaching across the community, so that there are no teachers per se, but rather a network of peers and mentors who coach one another. Such a distribution of teaching and mentoring roles has been documented in studies of children playing commercial games for fun at home (Ito et al., 2009; Stevens, Satwicz, and McCarthy, 2008). For example, Stevens, Satwicz, and McCarthy (2008) document siblings teaching each other as they play games, including situations in which a younger sibling serves as a key resource to help an older sibling pursue her goals in the game. Steinkuehler (2008) found that the ways in which massively multiplayer video games structure participation appears to foster the collaborative problem solving that is critical to learning in these games. To date, however, the design features that support these kinds of participation have not been sufficiently explored (Steinkuehler, 2005).

Differentiation of Roles and Expertise

A key opportunity for informal science education is to create contexts for collective participation without identical learning outcomes for each student (Collins and Halverson, 2009). Informal science learning contexts can support the co-construction of learning goals between learners and designers. Learners can—and should—have significant opportunities to pursue interests and develop unique identities as consumers and producers of information and as "professionals" in domains.

Research suggests that role-playing games are a good tool and context for creating such learning experiences. Shaffer (2006), for example, emphasizes the active nature of role play in extended games as players integrate knowledge, skills, attitudes, and identity under an "epistemic frame." In Schaffer's view, epistemic frames are the ways of knowing, of deciding what is worth knowing, and of adding to the collective body of knowledge and understanding in the virtual community of the game. As players confront increasingly challenging situations, they embark on trajectories from novices to experts. Notably, there is frequently no single model "expert" in a given game community but multiple ways that one can perform "being an expert" (Steinkuehler, 2006). In their most advanced forms, games frequently include opportunities for players to write about and within the game and support learning trajectories that lead toward legitimate participation in social relations beyond the game context itself.

Developing Science Literacy

Squire and Patterson (2009) propose that the use of games for informal science learning provides an important opportunity to improve the general scientific literacy of the population. They argue that understanding and responding to current social and scientific challenges (e.g., climate change, pandemics) requires ongoing attention to and understanding of scientific discoveries. It is no longer possible for citizens to learn all they need to know about science in school or in higher education. However, the rate of "scientific civic literacy" in the United States is barely 20 percent (Miller, Pardo, and Niwa, 1997). The definition of scientific civic literacy developed by Miller (1998) may be particularly useful for informal science educators seeking to design games around key problems (like pandemics) that mobilize a citizenry toward action. In this definition, scientific civic literacy requires

- an understanding of critical scientific concepts and constructs, such as ecosystems, the molecule, DNA;
- an understanding of the nature and process of scientific inquiry;
- a pattern of regular information consumption; and
- a disposition toward taking action to make change in one's lifestyle as necessary.

The weak state of current scientific civic literacy may suggest that the field of science education should increase its attention to the goal of developing citizens who are disposed toward actively engaging in civic affairs. There is reason to hope that digital games and simulations can help to advance this goal. In a recent survey of scientific civic literacy, the consumption of informal science materials (science magazines, television programs, books, science websites, museums) trailed only the completion of an undergraduate science course as a predictor of scientific civic literacy (Miller, 2001, 2002). The participatory nature of games, which is hypothesized to create dispositions toward taking action in the world (see Thomas and Brown, 2007), may be particularly well suited to fostering this disposition.

CONSTRAINTS OF INFORMAL SETTINGS

Social, Cultural, and Technical Constraints

Ito (2009) observes that gaming is predominantly a social and recreational activity and that any effort to introduce games designed for learning must consider the informal contexts that structure game play. As discussed below, these contexts influence children's and adolescents' access to games, the extent to which they play them, and the potential of games to support science learning.

One important context is everyday social play among local peers and siblings. Recent studies document that gaming is practically ubiquitous among U.S. children and teens and is associated more with social integration than isolation (Ito and Bittanti, 2009; Kahne, Middaugh, and Evans, 2009; Kutner and Olson, 2008). The research also shows that young people choose to play games that are popular among their peers and that recreational gaming is increasingly popular across genders and ages (Ito and Bittanti, 2009; Stevens, Satwicz, and McCarthy, 2008). Another context consists of intentional gaming clubs and communities, both online and local. Participants in intentional gaming constitute a minority of the larger universe of game players. They are usually boys and often distinguish themselves from more casual and recreational gamers as gamers or geeks. As noted above, these contexts support informal learning. Researchers have observed highly focused, interest-driven learning and creative production among these communities of intentional gamers (Ito and Bittanti, 2009).

For most children and youth, the context of family and home is the way in which they obtain access to gaming consoles, games, and the time and space to play them. Research on media access indicates that, while game consoles and entertainment titles are widely available, even in lower income homes, personal computers and learning software are not as widespread (Buckingham and Scanlon, 2002; Giacquinta, Bauer, and Levin, 1993; Roberts and Foehr, 2008). The presence of educational games or other types of learning software in their homes does not enhance the social standing of children and youth in their peer networks.

Although siblings and parents sometimes play together, they also compete for access to home entertainment resources, and most parents have established various rules and limits surrounding game play. Generally, both parents and children view gaming as an activity in opposition to academic learning (Buckingham, 2007; Horst, 2009; Ito and Bittanti, 2009; Stevens, Satwicz, and McCarthy, 2008). Such views, as well as the family's ability to pay for gaming technology and game titles, could constrain the potential of games to support shared learning within the family.

Finally, the commercial gaming industry is an important influence on recreational gaming that may constrain the potential of games to support science learning. Any effort to introduce games designed for informal science learning will have to compete with the production and marketing of commercial games for young people's attention. History has demonstrated the challenges of inserting learning software and educational agendas into practices already saturated with commercial media culture (Buckingham, 2007; Buckingham and Scanlon, 2002; Giacquinta, Bauer, and Levin, 1993; Ito, 2009; Seiter, 2005). While independent, educational, and civic games have been a marginal but persistent feature of the commercial games landscape, there is not yet a robust market for public interest games that is comparable to the market for television or radio.

Games as Enrichment Activities

Home and family contexts may encourage and/or constrain access to games and the use of games for science learning. Many parents support their children's informal science learning by bringing them to visit museums, zoos, aquariums or science centers, some of which charge admission. Such informal learning centers tally millions of visitors annually (National Research Council, 2009). Historically, parents have also viewed certain forms of gaming—such as *Chess* and *Scrabble*—as valuable enrichment activities. Such games are purchased by adults, are culturally validated as learning games, and supported though clubs and competitions. In the 1980s, many parents purchased—and encouraged their children to play—electronic learning games, under the rubric of "edutainment" that they similarly viewed as enrichment activities. Games such as *Civilization* or those under *The Sims* and Lucas Learning labels were entertainment-oriented but had a stamp of approval from parents and educators and often crossed over to the school and enrichment space (Ito, 2009).

Young children and some teens are open to adult guidance in such informal learning activities, and welcome parents' game purchases and encouragement in game play. For example, Klopfer (2008) describes the shared enthusiasm of parent-child pairs who participated in a mystery game workshop at the Boston Museum of Science. The activity included children of late elementary school age and young adolescents. However, parental involvement can have mixed effects on young people's interest in and use of games. Researchers have found that many children, as they enter their late elementary and teen years, become more resistant to adults dictating their media choices (Ito and Bittanti, 2009). This is why the edutainment market is largely targeted toward early childhood and why games with an explicit learning agenda have a hard time sustaining interest among older children and adolescents playing at home.[2] Furthermore, unlike mainstream recreational games, these enrichment-oriented games suffer from certain class associations and are culturally marked as more highbrow media forms. This means that any attempt to use this genre of games to support science learning must carefully consider issues of class distinction, accessibility, and status in childrens' peer cultures.

Studies of home and family dynamics have demonstrated that parental cultivation of enrichment activities is associated with middle-class parenting styles (Lareau, 2003; Seiter, 2007). As a result of these cultural stereotypes, games designed for science learning could potentially alienate certain populations of children and adolescents. In private homes, these kinds of socioeconomic and cultural distinctions are in full force, in contrast to the equalizing efforts made in public schools. After-school spaces and computer clubs can function as mediating contexts in broadening access to these enrichment-oriented genres of gaming.

---

[2]There are a few examples of educational games targeted to adolescents that have sold successfully (see Chapter 6).

Research Constraints

Squire and Patterson (2009) identified several constraints on research and development of simulations and games to support informal science learning. The unique qualities of informal science education, even in its most structured settings, frequently run counter to the assumptions of modern statistical methods used in education research. These qualities—including diverse, participant-driven learning goals, emphasis on developing participants' interest, and models of flexible participation—contrast sharply with education research methods focusing on uniform learning outcomes that are specified in advance, fidelity in implementing an educational intervention, and isolation of variables. A lack of assessment methods aligned with these unique features of informal learning environments also constrains research. For example, as noted above, some adolescents who voluntarily joined in several sessions of gaming using a modified version of *Civilization* resisted taking pretests and posttests (DeVane, Durga, and Squire, 2009). This problem has also been reported by other researchers investigating the use of games for learning (Hayes and King, 2009; Steinkuehler and King, 2009).

In response to these constraints, researchers studying the effectiveness of games for learning in informal settings have frequently preferred case studies or other methods that enable them to gain longitudinal data, understand the role of the participant in defining the learning experience, and examine how participants' identities are shaped beyond the learning experience. Although experiments are possible in informal learning environments, the importance of user choice in activities still creates challenges. It is difficult, for example, to administer a uniform task to multiple participants and expect meaningful results. However, the underlying logical problems of user-defined learning goals or uniformity of treatment still need to be addressed.

Development Constraints

One type of constraint on development of games for informal science learning arises from the constraints of formal classroom environments. This reflects the reality that most games focused on science learning have been developed for—and tested in—classrooms. Squire and Patterson (2009) illustrate this constraint through the example of the game *Resilient Planet* (see Box 4-1).

Resilient Planet appears capable of advancing many of the science learning goals outlined in Chapter 2, including the goal of motivation that is so critical in informal learning environments. It may generate excitement, interest, and motivation by leveraging the allure of underwater exploration. It may increase conceptual understanding, because players are required to construct arguments about the causes of various phenomena, such as declines

BOX 4-1
Operation: Resilient Planet

In *Resilient Planet*, a single player pilots a remote-operated vehicle through a three-dimensional underwater world (see Figure 4-2) to carry out a mission to protect endangered turtles. The player steers the vehicle to retrieve underwater cameras that provide information about the behavior of the turtles, including their proximity to an oil-drilling platform at different times. The information obtained is used to remove the platform, using explosives, at a time when the turtles will not be nearby. While carrying out the mission, the player gathers information about marine phenomena, conducts scientific experiments, collects animal observational data, and watches video from real *National Geographic* researchers. The game was developed by the JASON Project, a not-for-profit science education subsidiary of *National Geographic* and Filament Games. It is integrated into the JASON ecology curriculum (*Operation: Resilient Planet*) for grades 5-8.

In another mission, the goal is to understand the causes for dramatic shifts in shark and monk seal populations in Hawaii. The player first chooses whether to study sharks or seals at the Papahānaumokuākea Marine Sanctuary and then collects data for inclusion in a scientific argument. The data are chronologically displayed in a cartoon box. After several data items have been collected, the player organizes the information to make an argument and presents the argument to a virtual researcher. A cartoon scenario of the player interacting with the researcher transpires as a storyboard sequence that influences what happens next in the game. The player also listens to and reads information provided by other virtual researchers, who provide assistance in completing the mission.

in the population of monk seals. However, this game, like many educational games, was designed for use in schools. Reflecting the constraints of school settings, the game is relatively linear and lasts only a few hours (for example, the mission focusing on shark and monk seal populations lasts one hour). Although the designers included a "Free Dive" mode that allows learners to freely explore the underwater world, most players focus on carrying out the short missions. If it were designed specifically for informal environments,

FIGURE 4-2 *A remote-operated underwater vehicle in Operation: Resilient Planet.*
SOURCE: The JASON Project. Reprinted with permission.

Resilient Planet might include more open-ended game play, more collaborative problems, and enhanced ties outward from the game experience toward scientific communities of practice.

The Challenge of Integrating Interest and Learning

Perhaps the greatest potential constraint to development of games for informal science learning is the difficulty of integrating participants' interest and learning. Squire and Patterson (2009) suggest that the major challenge for game designers is to create learning experiences that leverage learners' interests and goals while also advancing science learning goals. Studies in the late 1990s of play with such games as *The Magic School Bus Explores the Human Body*, *DinoPark Tycoon*, and *The Island of Dr. Brain*, found that players rarely oriented to the scientific content of the game without the explicit intervention of an educationally minded adult. When played on their own, these games were absorbed into the dynamics of children's and adolescents' peer culture, and players were more focused on "beating" the game and playing with the special effects than engaging with the scientific content (Ito, 2009). The popular science focus of these games appeared more important for legitimizing the games in the eyes of parents, who then provided them to their children, than as a focus of interest for the children. Unlike more traditional media, games are highly responsive to player intentionality and context, and children can easily circumvent engagement with content when playing with an entertaining simulation or multimedia adventure.

ALTERNATIVE APPROACHES TO BRIDGING LEARNING ACROSS CONTEXTS

A Variety of Approaches

Researchers, game developers, and community leaders are developing and testing several approaches to addressing the constraints described above so that games can support learning across formal and informal contexts. For example, the development of games that can be easily accessed from the web using cell phones or other mobile devices may reduce the current technical, social, and cultural constraints on educational gaming in homes while also reducing technical constraints on classroom use (see Chapter 3). The number of web-based educational games is growing rapidly, opening the possibility of students using their cell phones to follow their particular science learning interests at any time or place (Osterweil, 2009; see Chapter 6).

At the same time, some games designed for formal environments are supporting learning outside the usual time and space of the science class-room. For example, Dede (2009b) reports that students using *River City* were eager to spend extra time playing the game during lunch hour or before or after school. He notes several challenges to assigning or allowing voluntary access to games or simulations introduced in school for use at home. First, as noted above, not all students have ready access to the technology infrastructure needed to access and play the game. In addition, if the game or simulation has multiple users, then the possibility exists of students engaging in inappropriate behavior when unsupervised (e.g., on-line bullying, swearing).

To address these problems, the developers restricted use of the *River City* curriculum to in-school settings (class, lunch period, before or after school) in which an adult was present as monitor. They also created an automated "swear checker" that would respond to the use of bad words in student chat, reminding them to watch their language. They provided teachers each morning with chat logs of their students from the previous day so that the teachers could closely monitor student activities to encourage appropriate, on-task behaviors (Clarke and Dede, 2009). Students quickly realized that they were more closely monitored in the multi-user virtual environment than in other types of project-based learning, in which the teacher could not closely supervise every group's work simultaneously.

Implementation of the Taiga Park curriculum in *Quest Atlantis* offers another approach to overcoming the constraints outlined above. Barab (2009) reports that all teachers using the curriculum are required to participate in online professional development to familiarize them with the technology, the range of learning opportunities in the curriculum, and the inquiry-based teaching approaches that are most likely to support successful implementation of the curriculum. Continued learning is supported through an online forum in which teachers can share experiences. Participating teachers register each child who interacts with the curriculum and obtains parental consent for the child's participation in the research associated with the curriculum. The registration process allows students to log on to a secure website and interact with the curriculum in the classroom (grades 4-8), at home, or in another informal setting. The curriculum has been successfully implemented in Boys and Girls Clubs and other after-school centers, as well as in classrooms.

In addition to the core learning activities, the curriculum includes a teacher toolkit and voluntary activities, such as architecture, capturing fish, and making music, designed to allow students to pursue individual interests. To date, the curriculum has over 45,000 registered users in the United States, Australia, Canada, Singapore, Uganda, and other countries.

Barab (2009) emphasized that learning gains demonstrated among young people who play *Taiga Park* are not realized because the game is fun to play. Instead, players are motivated to learn because they recognize that their actions have a significant impact on the virtual world and that what they know is directly related to what they are able to do and ultimately who they will become. They experience feelings of identity with their avatars and the larger virtual world. Many features of the game are designed to build identity and motivate knowledge-seeking. For example, a player "owns" pieces of evidence, such as a crumpled-up piece of paper with a picture illustrating why fish are dying, and players are required to take on the views of the different competing groups in the game (loggers, indigenous farmers) as they question characters in the game.

The Importance of Middle Space

Research to date suggests that "middle spaces," such as recreation centers and after-school programs, can play an important role in supporting the use of games for learning. These spaces are less rigid than formal classroom environments, avoiding some of the constraints identified in Table 4-1, but they provide more structure and support for learning than may be available in the home or another unstructured setting. As noted above, researchers have observed highly focused, interest-driven learning and creative production among intentional gaming communities (Ito and Bittanti, 2009). An after-school gaming club was the setting that DeVane, Durga, and Squire (2009) used to test a modified version of *Civilization*, finding that the game supported development of systemic thinking about ecology and economics.

Dede (2009c) also observes that school clubs offer fertile ground for science games and simulations. As discussed in the previous chapter, he notes that science games and simulations can motivate students by allowing them to modify the game and the learning experience, referred to as modding (Annetta et al., 2009).

Middle spaces can help to overcome the social, cultural, and technical constraints outlined above, engaging students from low-income families, in which parents are less likely to introduce enrichment activities at home (Ito, 2009). For example, the Digital Youth Network in Chicago is a hybrid digital literacy program that creates opportunities for urban youth to engage in learning environments that span both school and out-of-school contexts. The project provides access and training in the use of new media literacy tools, activities that require media literacy to accomplish goals, and a continuum of mentors (high school through professionals). At the middle school level, the program includes mandatory in-school media arts classes and optional after-school pods in which students may build on what they learn in school and identify skills of their choice to explore in depth. The high school component allows youth to focus their development on an individual medium; youth who excelled in the middle school program are given internship opportunities while serving as mentors for middle school students (Digital Youth Network, 2010).

Created as a design experiment, the Digital Youth Network includes an extensive program of research using a variety of qualitative and quantitative methods. Survey responses indicate that participants, by the end of sixth grade, report a greater diversity of technological fluency-building activities than a sample of middle school (grades 6-8) students in Silicon Valley who had high access to computing tools at school and at home. In addition, participants reported an increase from the beginning of sixth grade to the end of seventh grade in the number of software tools for which they felt they possessed an expertise and competency to teach others. After-school participation in the pods, defined as participating in one or two years of the after-school sessions, correlated with an increase in depth of knowledge. Among students who attended these sessions, increased pod participation resulted in much higher reported rates of completing media literacy activities (e.g., participating in an online forum) (Digital Youth Network, 2010).

An example of an online middle space is the learning community formed around the web-based programming environment *Scratch* (Resnick et al., 2009). Like the Digital Youth Network, the environment aims to actively engage young people in producing, not merely consuming, digital media.

It is designed to introduce young people to programming in a fun and engaging way by supporting many different types of projects (stories, games, animations), making it easy for players to personalize their projects (e.g., by importing photos), and encouraging online communication. The easy-to-use programming language allows participants to support, collaborate, and critique one another and build on one another's work. Since its May 2007 launch, the learning environment has attracted 632,877 registered users, and participants have uploaded over 1.3 million projects. The core game audience is between the ages of 8 and 16, including high concentrations of 13- and 14-year-olds (see http://stats.scratch.mit.edu/community).

CONCLUSIONS

Although there is considerable variation within formal and informal contexts for science learning, informal learning contexts overall differ from formal learning contexts overall in several respects.

Conclusion: *Informal science learning environments have a number of unique characteristics when compared with formal learning environments, including the freedom to pursue a wider variety of learning goals, a greater focus on increasing the learner's interest and excitement, opportunities for individualized learning, and more flexible time structures.*

Informal contexts for science learning with simulations and games are diverse, varying in terms of the physical setting, the social and cultural environment, the technology, and the degree to which interaction with a simulation or game is structured.

Conclusion: *Informal environments vary along a number of dimensions that influence their potential to support science learning, including the degree of structure, the setting, and the social and cultural relationships among participants, peers, and teachers or mentors. The evidence on how the unique features of informal environments—and the different dimensions in these environments—align with different science learning outcomes is underdeveloped.*

Researchers studying informal gaming have noted the development of learning communities, in which experienced players mentor novices. Learners in these communities value expertise more than players' background or formal educational credentials. Games designed for science learning could potentially distribute teaching across communities of learners in a similar way.

Conclusion: *Teachers, other mentors, and knowledgeable peers have crucial roles to support learners to appropriately engage with games and simulations. Games, particularly those that are multi-user, can shift the conventional definition of the role of the teacher. Players can learn from one another, seeking out advice, guidance, and tips from others engaged in game play. However, there has been limited research on the impact these kinds of interactions have on advancing the five science learning goals discussed in this report.*

Bridging formal and informal learning environments through game play provides a significant opportunity that can remove traditional barriers between school and out-of-school contexts. In the future, access to games via mobile devices will allow students to engage in science games in school, at home, and every place in between. Games and simulations have the potential to:

- Significantly increase the "time on task" aspect of learning.
- Provide new forms of engaging with science.
- Help show learners how science is relevant to their daily lives.
- Increase the transfer of learning by exposing the learner to knowledge in a different context.
- Provide opportunities for children to explore and develop "passion topics" that might serve as gateways to further science study.

The teacher or other mentor plays a critical role in helping students formalize the knowledge they develop through game play in informal settings.

Conclusion: *Games and simulations potentially can bridge multiple spaces— at home, on mobile devices, in informal learning environments, and in schools—and therefore have the potential to develop durable, transferable learning. However, much more research is needed to understand this potential and to develop coherent connections between these spaces.*

5

The Role of Simulations and Games in Science Assessment

As outlined in previous chapters, simulations and games can increase students' motivation for science learning, deepen their understanding of important science concepts, improve their science process skills, and advance other important learning goals. However, the rapid development of simulations and games for science learning has outpaced their grounding in theory and research on learning and assessment.

This chapter focuses on assessment of the learning outcomes of simulations and games and their potential to both assess and support student science learning. The first section uses the lens of contemporary assessment theory to identify weaknesses in the assessment of student learning resulting from interaction with simulations and games, as well as weaknesses of science assessment more generally. The next section focuses on the opportunities offered by simulations for enhanced assessment of science learning. The third section discusses similar opportunities for enhanced assessment offered by games. The fourth section describes social and technical challenges to using simulations and games to assess science learning and the research and development needed to address these challenges. The final section presents conclusions.

MEASUREMENT SCIENCE AND SCIENCE ASSESSMENT

The past two decades have seen rapid advances in the cognitive and measurement sciences and an increased awareness of their complementary strengths in understanding and appraising student learning. *Knowing What Students Know: The Science and Design of Educational Assessment*, a National Research Council report (2001), conceptualized the implications of the integration of these advances for assessment in the form of an "assessment triangle." This symbol represents the critical idea that assessment is a highly principled process of reasoning from evidence in which one attempts to infer what students know from their responses to carefully constructed and selected sets of tasks or performances. One corner of the triangle represents cognition (theory and data about how students learn), the second corner represents observations (the tasks students might perform to demonstrate their learning), and the third corner represents interpretation (the methods used to draw inferences from the observations). The study committee emphasized that the three elements of the triangle must be closely interrelated for assessment to be valid and informative.

Mislevy et al. (2003) extended this model in a framework known as evidence-centered design (ECD). This framework relates (1) the learning goals, as specified in a model of student cognition; (2) an evidence model specifying the student responses or performances that would represent the desired learning outcomes; and (3) a task model with specific types of questions or tasks designed to elicit the behaviors or performances identified in the evidence model (Messick, 1994). The assessment triangle and ECD frameworks can be used in a variety of ways, including evaluation of the quality and validity of particular assessments that have been used to appraise student learning for research or instructional purposes and to guide the design of new assessments. Examples of both applications are described below.

Limitations of Assessments Used to Evaluate Learning with Simulations and Games

Quellmalz, Timms, and Schneider (2009) used ECD (see Figure 5-1) as a framework to evaluate assessment practices used in recent research on science simulations. The authors reviewed 79 articles that investigated the use of simulations in grades 6-12 and included reports of measured learning outcomes, drawing on a study by Scalise et al. (2009).

The authors found that the assessments included in the research on student learning outcomes rarely reflected the integrated elements of this framework. The studies tended to not describe in detail the learning outcomes targeted by the simulation (the student model), how tasks were designed to provide evidence related to this model (the task and evidence models), or the approach used to interpret the evidence and reach conclusions about student performance (the interpretation component of the assessment triangle). The lack of attention to the desired learning outcomes led to a lack of alignment between the assessment tasks used and the capabilities of simulations. Simulations often engage students in science processes in virtual environments, presenting them with interactive tasks that yield rich streams of data. Although these data could provide evidence of science process skills

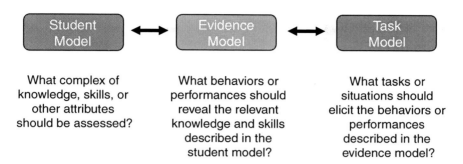

Student Model	⟷	Evidence Model	⟷	Task Model
What complex of knowledge, skills, or other attributes should be assessed?		What behaviors or performances should reveal the relevant knowledge and skills described in the student model?		What tasks or situations should elicit the behaviors or performances described in the evidence model?

FIGURE 5-1 *Evidence-centered design of assessments.*
SOURCE: Quellmalz et al. (2009). Reprinted with permission.

and other science learning goals that are difficult to measure via conventional items and tests, such data were rarely used for assessment purposes. Instead, most of the studies used paper and pencil tests to measure only one science learning goal—conceptual understanding.

The lack of description of the desired learning goals and how the tasks were related to these goals made it impossible to evaluate the depth of conceptual understanding or the nature of science process skills measured in the studies of simulations (Quellmalz, Timms, and Schneider, 2009). In addition, the limited descriptions of the assessment items and data on item and task quality made it impossible to evaluate the technical quality of the assessment items or their validity for drawing inferences about the efficacy of simulations to enhance student learning. Finally, the studies did not always describe how the assessment results could be used by researchers, teachers, or other potential users and for which user group the results might be most appropriate.

When Quellmalz, Timms, and Schneider (2009) applied the ECD framework to evaluate assessments of student outcomes in recent studies of games, they concluded that research on how to effectively assess the learning outcomes of playing games is still in its infancy. As was the case with simulations, the studies often failed to specify the desired learning outcomes or how assessment tasks and items have been designed to measure these outcomes. Furthermore, game developers and researchers rarely tapped the capacity of the technology to embed assessment and learning in game play.

In an education system driven by standards and external, large-scale assessments, simulations and games are unlikely to be more widely used until their capacity to advance science learning goals can be demonstrated via assessment results. Such results, in turn, will require alternate forms of evidence and improved assessment methods. At the same time, improved assessment methods that draw on the capabilities of simulations and games to measure important student learning outcomes have potential to address some of the major weaknesses of current science assessment, as discussed below.

Limitations of Assessments Used to Evaluate Science Learning

Most large-scale science assessment programs operated by states and school districts are largely incapable of measuring the multiple science learning goals that simulations and games support. The states administer summative assessments to measure student science achievement. These assessments reflect current state science standards, which frequently give greater weight to conceptual understanding than other learning goals and typically include long lists of science topics that students are expected to master each year[1] (Duschl, 2004; National Research Council, 2006). Although science standards in the majority of states also address science processes and understanding of the nature of science, they do not always explicitly describe the performances associated with meeting these learning goals, making it difficult to align assessments with these elements of the standards (National Research Council, 2006).

Most large-scale science assessments use paper and pencil formats and are composed primarily of selected-response (multiple-choice) tasks, making them well suited to testing student knowledge of the many content topics included in state science standards. Although they can provide a snapshot of some science process skills, they do not adequately measure others, such as formulating scientific explanations or communicating scientific understanding (Quellmalz et al., 2005). They cannot assess students' ability to design and execute all of the steps involved in carrying out a scientific investigation (National Research Council, 2006). A few states have developed standardized classroom assessments of science process skills, providing uniform kits of materials that students use to carry out hands-on laboratory tasks; this approach has also been used in the National Assessment of Educational Progress (NAEP) science test. However, because administering and scoring the hands-on tasks can be cumbersome and expensive, this approach is rarely used in state achievement tests (National Research Council, 2005b).

Another problem of current science assessment is its lack of coherence as a system (National Research Council, 2005b, 2006). Although states and school districts use summative assessments to evaluate overall levels of student science achievement, teachers use formative assessments to provide diagnostic

---

[1]A National Research Council committee is currently developing a framework for new science standards that will focus on a smaller number of "big ideas" in science.

feedback during instruction, so that teaching and learning can be adapted to meet student needs. In most states and school districts, these different types and levels of science assessment are designed and administered separately. Often they are not well aligned with each other, nor are they linked closely with curriculum and instruction to advance the science learning goals specified in state science standards. As a result, the multiple forms and levels of assessment results can yield conflicting or incomplete information about student science learning (National Research Council, 2006).

Despite repeated calls for improvement (National Research Council, 2005b, 2006, 2007), science assessment has been slow to change. Simulations and games offer new possibilities for improvement in the assessment of critical forms of knowledge and skill that are deemed to be important targets for science learning (National Research Council, 2007). As such, both science learning and assessment stand to benefit from tapping the possibilities offered by simulations and games.

ASSESSMENT OPPORTUNITIES IN SIMULATIONS

New Paradigms in Large-Scale Summative Assessment

A new generation of assessments is attempting to break the mold of traditional, large-scale summative testing practices through the use of current technology and media (Quellmalz, Timms, and Schneider, 2009). Simulations are being designed to measure deep conceptual understanding and science process skills that are difficult to assess using paper and pencil tests or hands-on laboratory tasks. This new paradigm in assessment design and use aims to align summative assessment more closely to the processes and contexts of learning and instruction, particularly in science (Quellmalz and Pellegrino, 2009).

By allowing learners to interact with representations of phenomena, simulations expand the range of situations that can be used to provide interesting and challenging problems to be solved. This, in turn, allows testing of conceptual understanding and science process skills that are not tested well or at all in a static format. Simulations also allow adaptive testing that adjusts the items or tasks presented based on the learner's responses, and the creation of logs of learners' problem-solving sequences as they investigate scientific phenomena. Finally, because simulations use multiple modalities to represent science systems and to elicit student responses, English language learners, students with disabilities, and low-performing students may be better able to demonstrate their knowledge and skills through simulations than when responding to text-laden print tests (Kopriva, Gabel, and Bauman, 2009).

The use of short simulation scenarios in large-scale summative assessments is increasing in national, international, and state science testing programs (see Box 5-1). These examples demonstrate the capacity of simulations to generate evidence of students' summative science achievement levels, including measures of science process skills and other science learning goals seldom tapped in paper-based tests (Quellmalz and Pellegrino, 2009).

New Paradigms in Integrating Assessment with Instruction

Formative assessments are intended to measure student progress during instruction, providing timely feedback to support learning. Simulations are well suited to the data collection, complex analysis, and individualized feedback needed for formative assessment (Brown, Hinze, and Pellegrino, 2008). They can be used to collect evidence related to students' inquiry approaches and strategies, reflected in the features of the virtual laboratory tools they manipulate, the information they select, the sequence and number of trials they attempt, and the time they allocate to different activities. Simulations can also provide adaptive tasks, reflecting student responses, as well as immediate, individualized feedback and customized, graduated coaching. Technology can be used to overcome constraints to the systematic use of formative assessment in the classroom, allowing measurement of skills and deep understandings in a feasible and cost-effective manner (Quellmalz and Haertel, 2004).

Reflecting their potential to support both formative and summative assessment, simulations and games offer the possibility of designing digital and mixed media curricula that integrate assessment with instruction.

An Example of an Integrated Science Learning Environment

SimScientists is an ongoing program of research and development focusing on the use of simulations as environments for formative and summative assessment and as curriculum modules to supplement science instruction (Quellmalz et al, 2008). One of these projects, Calipers II, provides an example of this type of integrated digital learning environment (Quellmalz, Timms, and Buckley, in press). It is a simulation-based curriculum unit that embeds a sequence of assessments designed to measure student understanding of components of an ecosystem and roles of organisms in it, interactions in the ecosystem, and the emergent behaviors that result from these interactions (Buckley et al., 2009).

The summative assessment is designed to provide evidence of middle school students' understanding of ecosystems and inquiry practices after completion of the curriculum unit on ecosystems. Students are presented with the overarching problem of preparing a report describing an Australian grassland ecosystem for an interpretive center. Working with simulations, they investigate the roles and relationships of the animals, birds, insects, and grass in the ecosystem by observing animations of the interactions of these

BOX 5-1
Technology-Based Science Assessment in
Large-Scale Assessment Programs

Information and communications technologies expand the range of knowledge and cognitive skills that can be assessed beyond what is measured in conventional paper and pencil tests. The computer's ability to capture student inputs while he or she is performing complex, interactive tasks permits the collection of evidence of such processes as problem solving and strategy use as reflected by the information selected, numbers of attempts, and time allocation. Such data can be combined with statistical and measurement algorithms to extract patterns associated with varying levels of expertise. In addition, technology can be used for adaptive testing that integrates diagnosis of errors with student and teacher feedback.

Propelled by these trends, technology-based science tests are increasingly appearing in state, national, and international testing programs. The area of science assessment is perhaps leading the way in exploring the presentation and interpretation of complex, multifaceted problem types and assessment approaches. In 2006 and 2009, the Programme for International Student Assessment pilot-tested the Computer-Based Assessment of Science (CBAS), designed to measure science knowledge and inquiry processes not assessed in paper-based test booklets. CBAS tasks include scenario-based item and task sets, such as investigations of the temperature and pressure settings for a simulated nuclear reactor.

The 2009 National Assessment of Educational Progress (NAEP) science test included Interactive Computer Tasks designed to test students' ability to engage in science inquiry practices. These simulation-based tasks measure scientific understanding and inquiry skills more accurately than do paper and pencil tests. The 2012 NAEP Technological Literacy Assessment will include simulations designed to assess how well students can use information and communications technology tools and their ability to engage in the engineering design process. At the state level, Minnesota has an online science test with tasks engaging students in simulated laboratory experiments or investigations of such phenomena as weather and the solar system.

Bennett et al. (2007) pioneered the design of simulation-based assessment tasks that were included in the 2009 NAEP science test. In one such task, the students were presented with a scenario involving a helium balloon and asked to determine how different payload masses affect the altitude of the balloon. They could design a virtual experiment, manipulate parameters, run their experiment, record their data, and graph the results. The students could obtain various types of data and plot their relationships before reaching a conclusion and typing in a final response.

SOURCE: Adapted from Quellmalz and Pellegrino (2009).

organisms. In one task, students draw a food web representing interactions among the organisms in the ecosystem (see Figure 5-2). Students then conduct investigations with the simulation to predict, observe, and explain what happens to population levels when the numbers of particular organisms are varied (see Figure 5-3). In a culminating task, students present their findings about the grasslands ecosystem.

To assess transfer of learning, the curriculum unit engages students with a companion simulation focusing on a different ecosystem (a mountain lake). Formative assessment tasks embedded in this simulation identify the types of errors individual students make, and the system follows up with feedback and graduated coaching. The levels of feedback and coaching progress from notifying the student that an error has occurred and asking him or her to try again, to showing results of investigations that met the specifications.

The new curriculum unit shows promise in addressing two weaknesses of current science assessment. First, it assesses science process skills as well as other learning goals beyond the science content emphasized in current science tests. Second, it is designed to increase coherence in assessment systems. The researchers are collaborating with several state departments of education to integrate the assessments into classroom-level formative assessment and district- and state-level summative assessment. The goal is

FIGURE 5-2 *Screenshot of SimScientists Ecosystems Benchmark Assessment showing a food web diagram produced by a student.*
SOURCE: Quellmalz, Timms, and Schneider (2009). Reprinted with permission.

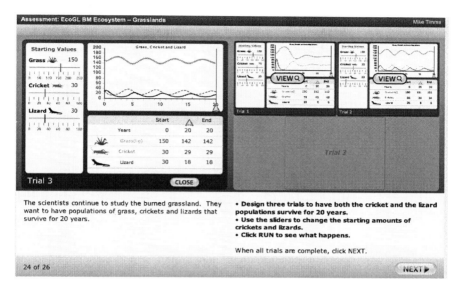

FIGURE 5-3 *Screenshot of SimScientists Ecosystems Benchmark Assessment showing a student's investigations with the interactive population model.*
SOURCE: Quellmalz, Timms, and Schneider (2009). Reprinted with permission.

to create balanced systems in which district, classroom, and state tests are nested, mutually informed, and aligned.

An Example of an Integrated Environment for Problem Solving

Another example of assessment embedded in a simulation-based learning environment illustrates how the resulting data on student learning can be made useful and accessible in the classroom (Stevens, Beal, and Sprang, 2009). *Interactive Multimedia Exercises* (*IMMEX*) is an online library of science simulations that incorporate assessment of students' problem-solving performance, progress, and retention. Each problem set presents authentic real-world situations that require complex thinking. Originally created for use in medical school, *IMMEX* has been used to develop and assess science problem solving among middle, high school, and undergraduate science students as well as medical students.

One *IMMEX* problem set, *Hazmat*, asks students to use multiple chemical and physical tests to identify an unknown toxic spill. The learning environment randomly presents 39 different problem cases that require students to identify an unknown compound and tracks their actions and strategies as they gather information and solve the problems. Simple measures provide information on whether students solved the problem and the time required to reach the solution. More sophisticated measures assess students' strategies as they navigate the problem-solving tasks, and the two types of measures are combined to create learning trajectories.

As students of various ages work in *IMMEX*, they typically develop a consistent strategy after they have encountered a particular problem approximately four times (Cooper and Stevens, 2008). They tend to persist in this strategy over time, and their strategies are highly influenced by the teacher's model of problem solving. To help teachers intervene quickly and assist students in developing efficient, effective problem-solving strategies, *IMMEX* developers have created an online "digital dashboard." It provides whole-class information so that the teacher can compare progress across classes, and it also graphically displays the distribution of individual student performances in each class. The teacher may respond to the information by providing differentiated instruction to individual students, groups of students, or entire classes before asking them to continue solving problems. This example illustrates the potential of simulations to facilitate formative assessment by rapidly providing feedback that teachers can use to tailor instruction to meet individual learning needs.

ASSESSMENT OPPORTUNITIES IN GAMES

Although assessment of the learning outcomes of games is still at an early stage, work is under way to embed assessment in games in ways that support both assessment and learning. Quellmalz, Timms, and Schneider (2009) illustrate both the weakness of current assessment methods and these new opportunities by examining three games designed for science learning: *Quest Atlantis: Taiga Park*, *River City*, and *Crystal Island*. None of these games currently incorporates assessments of learning as core game play elements, but researchers are beginning to conceptualize, develop, and integrate dynamic assessment tasks in each one. The three games, which take a similar approach to immersing learners in simulated investigations, are not meant to represent the entire field of serious science games.

In *Quest Atlantis: Taiga Park*, students engage with virtual characters and data in order to evaluate competing explanations for declining fish populations in the Taiga River. Currently, assessment of learning in the game is undertaken by classroom teachers who score the written mission reports submitted by students (Hickey, Ingram-Goble, and Jameson, 2009). Shute et al. (2009) propose to develop "stealth" assessment in *Taiga Park,* embedding performance tasks so seamlessly within game play that they are not noticed by the student playing the game. The proposed approach, which would allow monitoring of student progress and drive automated feedback to students, requires much further research, development, and validation.

In the game-based curriculum unit *River City,* students conduct virtual investigations to identify the cause of an illness and recommend strategies to combat it (Nelson, 2007; see Chapter 3). Most assessment is undertaken by teachers, who use rubrics to score each student's final written product—a recommendation letter to the mayor of River City. *River City* also engages students in self-assessment, as teams compare their research findings with those of other teams in their class. The game also incorporates some digital assessment, implemented in an embedded individualized guidance system that uses interaction histories to offer real-time, customized support for students' investigations. Nelson (2007) found a statistically positive relationship between levels of use of the guidance system and students' gain scores on a test of content knowledge. On average, boys used the guidance system less and performed more poorly in comparison to girls.

Crystal Island is a narrative-centered learning environment built on a commercial game platform. In this virtual world, students play the role of Alyx, the protagonist who is trying to discover the identity and source of an unidentified infectious disease. Students move their avatar around the island, manipulating objects, taking notes, viewing posters, operating lab equipment, and talking with nonplayer characters to gather clues about the disease's source. To progress through the mystery, students must form questions, generate hypotheses, collect data, and test their hypotheses. Students encounter five different problems related to diseases and finally select an appropriate treatment plan for the sickened researchers.

Assessment in *Crystal Island* is evolving. Currently it is mainly embedded in the reaction of in-game characters to the student's avatar. Researchers have been gradually building pedagogical agents into the game that attempt to gauge the student's emotional state while learning (anger, anxiety, boredom, confusion, delight, excitement, flow, frustration, sadness, fear) and react with appropriate empathy to support the student's problem-solving activities (McQuiggan, Robison, and Lester, 2008; Robison, McQuiggan, and Lester, 2009). Students playing this game take notes as they navigate through the virtual world, trying to identify the cause of a disease. Researchers scored these notes, using rubrics to place each student's notes into one of five categories representing progressively higher levels of science content knowledge and inquiry skills (McQuiggan, Robison, and Lester, 2008). For example, students whose notes included a hypothesis about the problem performed better on the posttests of content knowledge, so these notes were placed in a higher category than notes that did not include a hypothesis. Although the scoring process was time-consuming, it illuminated the importance of scaffolding students in their efforts to generate hypotheses.

McQuiggan, Robison, and Lester (2008) investigated whether machine learning techniques could be applied to create measurement models that use information from student notes to successfully predict the note-taking categories as judged by human scorers. Their research indicates that Bayes nets and other methods (discussed further below) could be applied to score student notes in real time. Application of such methods would reduce the costs of a scoring system that provides evidence of students' conceptual understanding and science process skills—skills that are difficult to measure using paper and pencil tests.

These three examples suggest that researchers and game developers are making some progress toward improved assessment of student learning as a result of game play activity, as well as assessment within game play to support better overall student learning. In her proposal to use evidence-centered assessment as a framework for assessment design in *Crystal Island,* Shute et al. (2009) recognizes the importance of clearly specifying desired learning outcomes and designing assessment tasks to provide evidence related to these outcomes. Nelson (2007) provides evidence that carefully designed embedded assessment in *River City* supports development of conceptual understanding. And the work on *Crystal Island* shows the potential of carefully designed assessment methods (in this case, scoring of student notes) to yield information that can inform design of online learning environments to support development of science process skills. The work also shows the potential of new measurement methods to draw inferences about student science learning from patterns derived from the extensive data generated by students' interactions with the characters, contexts, and scenarios that are found in games (McQuiggan, Robison, and Lester, 2008).

Another example of current efforts to integrate learning and assessment is provided by the Cisco Networking Academy, a global education program that teaches students how to design, build, troubleshoot, and secure computer networks. The academy's online training curriculum uses simulations and games. Behrens (2009) notes that, historically, the developers of the training curriculum created content that was loaded into a media shell for students to navigate. The software architecture of the curriculum was separate from that of the assessment system, even though the curriculum included embedded quizzes and simulation software (Frezzo, Behrens, and Mislevy, in press). More recently, the developers have begun to transfer performance data from the simulation activities in the curriculum to a business intelligence dashboard that would help instructors and students make sense of the large amount of performance data that is generated by the students' interactions with the simulation. Current research and development aims to make assessment a ubiquitous, unobtrusive element that supports learning in the digital learning environment.

SOCIAL AND TECHNICAL CHALLENGES

Social Challenges

The costs of new forms of assessment embedded in simulations and games could present a challenge to their wider use. Selected-response items, like those used in current large-scale science tests, can be scored by computer and are relatively inexpensive (National Research Council, 2002). Tests incorporating open-ended items that must be scored by humans are much more expensive to develop and score (Hamilton, 2003), although progress is being made in machine scoring of more complex test items. The states might be able to reduce the costs of new types of assessments by sharing assessment and task designs as well as data and reporting infrastructure. The current development of state assessment consortia, in response to the U.S. Department of Education's Race to The Top initiative to develop a new generation of high-stakes assessments, offers a vehicle for sharing the costs of all types of assessments, including ones designed to be used in simulation or gaming environments.

Another challenge is related to the role of the teacher. As mentioned previously, the teacher plays an important role in both supporting and assessing learning through simulations and games. While assessments embedded in simulations and games can provide timely, useful information to guide instruction, the extent to which a teacher uses this information may strongly influence how much learning takes place. If assessment were more widely incorporated in simulations and games, a large-scale teacher professional development effort would be needed to support and assist teachers in making use of the new information on individual students' progress. Teachers could be provided with instruction and practice related to how to use simulations and games for teaching as well as for aligned assessment purposes. At the same time, developers would need to consider how to make the assessment information most useful for teachers—as the developers of *IMMEX* have done in creating the online digital dashboard. The Cisco Networking Academy includes a comprehensive assessment authoring interface that allows instructors both to use simulation-based assessment and to customize or create their own assessment items.

Technical Challenges and Emerging Solutions

Perhaps the most important technical challenge to embedding assessment in simulations and games is how to make use of the rich stream of data and complex patterns generated as learners interact with these technologies to reliably and validly interpret their learning. Simulations and games engage learners in complex tasks. As defined by Williamson, Bejar, and Mislevy (2006), complex tasks have four characteristics:

1. Completion of the task requires the student to undergo multiple, nontrivial, domain-relevant steps or cognitive processes. For example, as shown in Figures 5-2 and 5-3, students in the SimScientists assessment first observe a simulated ecosystem, noting the behaviors of the organisms, then construct a food web to represent their observations, and finally use a population model tool to vary the number of organisms in the ecosystem and observe outcomes over time.

2. Multiple elements, or features, of each task performance are captured and considered to determine the summative performance or provide diagnostic feedback. Simulations and games are able to do this, capturing a wide range of student responses and actions, from standard multiple-choice tasks and short written responses to actions like gathering quantitative evidence on fish, water, and sediment in a lake (Squire and Jan, 2007).

3. There is a high degree of potential variability in the types of data provided for each task, reflecting the relatively unconstrained learning activities in simulations and games. For example, some simulations include measures of the time taken by a student to perform a task, but the amount of time spent does not necessarily reflect more or less effective performance. Without being considered in conjunction with additional variables about task performance, time is not an easy variable to interpret.

4. The measurement of the adequacy of task solutions requires the task features to be considered as an interdependent set, rather than as conditionally independent. Simulations and games can mimic real-world scenarios and thereby provide greater authenticity to the assessment, which in turn would impact its potential validity. At the same time, however, the use of these complex tasks reduces the number of measures that can be included in any one test, thereby reducing reliability as typically construed in large-scale testing contexts.

As illustrated by these four characteristics, engaging students in complex tasks yields diverse sequences of student behaviors and performances. Assessment requires drawing inferences in real time about student learning from these diverse behaviors and performances. However, most conventional psychometric theory and methods are not well suited for such modeling and interpretation. To overcome these limitations, researchers are pursuing a variety of applications of current methods, such as item response theory (IRT), while also exploring new methods better suited to modeling assessment data derived from complex tasks. Such new methods can accommodate uncertainty about the current state of the learner, model patterns of student behavior, and be used to provide the basis for immediate feedback during task performance (Quellmalz, Timms, and Schneider, 2009).

IRT is one existing method often used for conventional large-scale tests that shows promise for application to assessment of learning with games and simulations. IRT models place estimates of student ability and item difficulty on the same linear scale, so that the difference between a student's ability estimate and the item difficulty can be used to interpret student performance. This method could be useful in determining how much help students need when solving problems in an intelligent learning environment, by measuring the gap between item difficulty and current learner ability (Timms, 2007). In a study of *IMMEX*, Stevens, Beal, and Sprang (2009) used IRT analysis to distinguish weaker from stronger problem solvers among 1,650 chemistry students using the *Hazmat* problem set. The IRT analysis informed further research in which the authors compared the different learning strategies of weaker and stronger problem solvers in several different classrooms and tested interventions designed to improve students' problem solving.

Researchers are also applying and testing machine learning methods[2] to allow computers to infer behavior patterns based on the large amounts of data generated by students' interactions with simulations and games. One promising method is the Bayes net (also called a Bayesian network). The use of Bayes nets in assessment, including assessment in simulations and games, has grown (Martin and VanLehn, 1995; Mislevy and Gitomer, 1996). For example, Bayes nets are used to score the ecosystems benchmark assessments in SimScientists, and Cisco Networking Academy staff have used this method to assess examinees' ability to design and troubleshoot computer networks (Behrens et al., 2008).

Another promising machine learning method is the Artificial Neural Network (ANN). The detailed assessments of the quality of student problem solving in *IMMEX* are enabled by ANN, together with other techniques (Stevens, Beal, and Sprang, 2009).

In addition to machine learning methods, developers sometimes use simpler, rule-based methods to provide immediate assessment and feedback in response to student actions in the simulation or game. Rule-based methods employ some type of logic to decide how to interpret a student action. A simple example would be posing a multiple-choice question in which the distracters (wrong answer choices) were derived from known misconceptions in the content being assessed. The student's incorrect response revealing a misconception could be diagnosed logically and immediate action could be taken, such as providing coaching.

---

[2]More information on machine learning is available in Mitchell (1997) and Bishop (2006).

Research and Development Needs

Applications of the new methods described in this chapter offer promise to strengthen assessment of the learning outcomes of simulations and games and to seamlessly embed assessment in them in ways that support science teaching and learning. Wider use of the ECD framework would encourage researchers, measurement specialists, and developers to explicitly describe the intended learning goals of a simulation or game and how tasks and items were designed to measure those goals. This, in turn, could support an increased focus on science process skills and other learning outcomes that are often targeted by simulations and games but have rarely been measured to date, strengthening the field of science assessment. Behrens (2009) cautions that, without greater clarity about intended learning outcomes, designers may add complex features to simulations and games that have no purpose. He suggests that the "physical" modeling of a game or simulation will need to evolve simultaneously with modeling of the motivation and thinking of the learner.

Perhaps the greatest technical challenge to embedding assessment of learning into simulations and games lies in drawing inferences from the large amount of data created by student interactions with these learning environments. Further research is needed in machine learning and probability-based test development methods and their application. Such research can help to realize these technologies' potential to seamlessly integrate learning and assessment into engaging, motivating learning environments. Research and development projects related to games would be most effective if they coordinated assessment research with game design research. Such projects could help realize the potential of assessments to motivate and direct the learner to specific experiences in the game that are appropriate to individual science learning needs.

Continued research and development is critical to improve assessment of the learning outcomes of simulations and games. Improved assessments are needed for research purposes—to more clearly demonstrate the effectiveness of simulations and games to advance various science learning goals—and for teaching and learning. Continued research and development of promising approaches that embed assessment and learning scaffolds directly into simulations and games holds promise to strengthen science assessment and support science learning. Recognizing the need for further research to fulfill this promise, the U.S. Department of Education's draft National Education Technology Plan (2010, p. xiii) calls on states, districts, the federal government, and other educational stakeholders to:

> Conduct research and development that explore how gaming technology, simulations, collaboration environments, and virtual worlds can be used in assessments to engage and motivate learners and to assess complex skills and performances embedded in standards.

CONCLUSIONS

The rapid development of simulations and games for science learning has outpaced their grounding in theory and research on learning and assessment. Recent research on simulations uses assessments that are not well aligned with the capacity of these technologies to advance multiple science learning goals. More generally, state and district science assessment programs are largely incapable of measuring the multiple science learning goals that simulations and games support. However, a new generation of assessments is attempting to use technology to break the mold of traditional, large-scale summative testing practices. Science assessment is leading the way in exploring the presentation and interpretation of complex, multifaceted problem types and assessment approaches.

Conclusion: *Games and simulations hold enormous promise as a means for measuring important aspects of science learning that have otherwise proven challenging to assess in both large-scale and classroom testing contexts. Work is currently under way that provides examples of the use of simulations for purposes that include both formative and summative assessment in classrooms and large-scale testing programs, such as NAEP and PISA.*

In an education system driven by standards and external, large-scale assessments, simulations and games are unlikely to be more widely used until their capacity to advance multiple science learning goals can be demonstrated via assessment results. This chapter provides examples of current work to provide such summative assessment results, by embedding assessment in game play. These examples suggest that it is valuable to clearly specify the desired learning outcomes of a game, so that assessment tasks can be designed to provide evidence aligned with these learning outcomes. They also illuminate the potential of new measurement methods to draw inferences about student science learning from the extensive data generated by students' interactions with the games—for the purpose of both summative and formative assessment.

Conclusion: *Games will not be useful as alternative environments for formative and summative assessment until assessment tasks can be embedded effectively and unobtrusively into them. Three design principles may aid this process. First, it is important to establish learning goals at the outset of game design, to ensure that the game play supports these goals. Second, the design should include assessment of performance at key points in the game and use the resulting information to move the player to the most appropriate level of the game to support individual learning. In this way, game play, assessment, and learning are intertwined. Third, the extensive data generated by a* *learner's interaction with the game should be used for summative as well as formative purposes, to measure the extent to which a student has advanced in the targeted science learning goals because of game play.*

Research on how to effectively assess the learning outcomes of playing games is still in its infancy. Investigators are beginning to explore how best to embed assessment in games in ways that support both assessment and learning.

Conclusion: *Although games offer an opportunity to enhance students' learning of complex science principles, research on how to effectively assess their learning and use that information in game environments to impact the learning process is still in its infancy.*

Continued research and development is critical to improve assessment of the learning outcomes of simulations and games. Improved assessments are needed for research purposes—to more clearly demonstrate the effectiveness of simulations and games to advance various science learning goals—and to support improvements in teaching and learning.

Conclusion: *Much further research and development is needed to improve assessment of the science learning outcomes of simulations and games and realize their potential to strengthen science assessment more generally and support science learning.*

6

Bringing Simulations and Games to Scale

This chapter considers the potential to scale up the use of simulations and games for science learning. The first section provides an overview of current market penetration of games in formal and informal learning contexts and identifies barriers to increased distribution and sales. The second section discusses alternative future pathways to scale. Although the chapter primarily focuses on games, the scaling issues are relevant to simulations as well. The chapter ends with conclusions.

BARRIERS TO SCALE

Increasing the uptake of games for science learning is a complex problem affected by a variety of barriers to use in both the formal context of the science classroom and the informal context of the home, science museum, or after-school club. Some barriers, such as the lack of viable business models and inadequate attention to consumer testing, limit development and sales of games in both formal and informal learning contexts. At the same time, there are barriers to marketing educational games that are unique to formal education. Educational markets for games are fundamentally different from broader public markets. It is important to keep in mind that blockbuster sales of commercial games establish a bar that has never been achieved by any educational software product. For example, *World of Warcraft—Wrath of the Lich King* sold 2.8 million copies within 24 hours of its November 2008 release.

The Lack of Proven Business Models

Mayo (2009b) argues that the primary barrier to wider use of science games is the lack of a successful business model.

One business model, in which academic developers aim to commercialize a game, generally fails for one of two reasons, in Mayo's (2009b) view. The first reason is that grants provided for game development generally do not include funding for commercial "hardening" (enhancing security, consumer testing, refining), marketing, and distribution. Second, even if the funders do support these activities, most academic developers lack the skills and knowledge, personnel, and financial resources to harden and market the game. In addition, academic reward systems typically do not encourage faculty members to commercialize educational games.

A representative of the commercial game industry (Gershenfeld, 2009) agreed with Mayo that most academic game developers lack the expertise needed to commercialize games. He argued that educational games have not sold well because academic developers have not designed them from the beginning to successfully meet market demand, as commercial publishers do. Publishers have staff and expertise to support the entire life cycle of a game, including marketing, distribution, and business development (see Box 6-1).

Another business model has also failed to gain traction in Mayo's (2009b) view. In this model, a large commercial gaming company with knowledge, investment capital, and marketing expertise would develop and market games for science learning. However, the typical business model of entertainment companies—an enormous up-front investment in game development, including high-quality graphics, followed by millions of sales to individuals within a few months of release—is not aligned with educational markets. Entertainment companies are not familiar with educational markets or how best to market to them, and they may not view these markets as potentially profitable. Uncertain about the potential sales revenue of educational games, these companies have made few efforts to develop educational games and have not established distribution channels to market them, either to schools or to the public.

A variation of this model would tap the knowledge and marketing expertise of textbook publishers as a way to develop and distribute science games. However, these companies' systems for selling print books—including their sales incentives and outreach to state textbook adoption committees—are poorly suited to marketing learning games. Textbook publishers generally focus on selling textbook editions that may remain unchanged for up to six years, but computer operating systems and software are revised frequently, so an educational game requires ongoing maintenance and upgrading. For all these reasons, efforts to market serious games through commercial textbook publishing companies have faltered.

BOX 6-1
Designing Games for Consumer Acceptance

Some observers attribute the limited sales of educational games to date to the lack of a commercial-quality example or market leader (Mayo, 2009b). Most educational games are produced for less than $1 million, while commercial games often cost $10-$100 million. A Sony Corporation executive (Hight, 2009) observed that, in the world of commercial gaming, graphics are very important. In 2009, half of his 135-person team working on the game *God of War 3* was devoted to creating detailed three-dimensional graphics (the total project budget was over $40 million).

Mayo (2009b) argued that such large investments in graphics may not be necessary for consumer acceptance of educational games. She noted that *Whyville* has attracted 5 million regular players, although it cost only $30,000 to develop and incorporates simple two-dimensional graphics.* The Sony representative (Hight, 2009) agreed, noting that commercial publishers look for a variety of other attributes—besides expensive, detailed graphics—when considering the potential audience appeal of a game. He said that a coherent artistic vision throughout the game is very important, as illustrated by the small, web-based game *flOw,* created by a university student as a master of fine arts project. Hight invested less than $500,000 to purchase and market the game, which is sold on line through the PlayStation Network. He observed that game distribution channels are beginning to move beyond a handful of large retailers, which will accept only a few new game titles each year due to their limited shelf space. Games are increasingly marketed directly to consumers on the web—a trend that facilitates sales of inexpensive games (including educational games) in niche markets. At the same time, new authoring tools are reducing the costs of graphics design (Mayo, 2009b).

A key element in design for consumer acceptance is to repeatedly test the game's acceptance by the target audience (Gershenfeld, 2009). Hight (2009) noted that Sony game development teams invite young people (the target audience) to play games in a special room, where their facial expressions and the content on the screen are recorded. Experts thoroughly observe the players as they navigate through every stage of the game, taking notes on what the players do and do not understand and when the players are enjoying themselves. Extensive testing is important because potential customers can be very quickly turned off (within 15 seconds) by a weak interface. This extensive consumer testing during the development process is likely to be as important with educational games as it has proven to be with purely commercial games.

---

*There is some evidence that idealized graphics are more effective than highly realistic graphics in facilitating science learning and transfer of learning across domains (Son and Goldstone, 2009; see Chapter 2).

Marketing Barriers in K-12 Education

In interviews, executives of companies engaged in developing and marketing educational games identified major barriers to marketing educational games to schools and school districts (Mayo, 2009b). Although most of the games discussed in these interviews do not focus specifically on science learning, the barriers identified are directly relevant to science games.

The executives pointed to a lack of distribution channels as the primary barrier to successfully marketing games in K-12 education. They emphasized the challenges to reach a point of purchase, noting that it is difficult, labor-intensive work to market games to schools and school districts. This work has included a variety of marketing approaches. Officials of two companies reported marketing games directly to teachers, approaching them through teacher conferences and websites. Teachers have purchased both individual games and classroom site licenses, using classroom supplies budgets and their own personal funds. However, one company found it more profitable to target school districts, marketing to curriculum coordinators and instructional designers with access to state and federal funding sources. Although the company experienced lengthy waits before licenses were purchased, the licenses were profitable and tended to be renewed for many years.

Another approach is to bundle a game with teacher professional development. One company has partially supported an educational game through sales of professional development classes, providing the game as part of the total package. In another approach, Numedeon, Inc. marketed the game *Whyville* directly to students at home, encouraging them to play the game and engage their class. In this case, no purchase was necessary, as the game is free to all users. Finally, the Kauffman Foundation has distributed educational games to schools by encouraging game developers to place older or demonstration versions of their games on state-financed laptops distributed to middle school students in Maine and Michigan. The developers obtained free exposure and potential sales for commercial variations of the same games.

The executives observed that, even if this primary barrier can be overcome and distribution channels are successfully established, several other barriers may limit the use of games in schools (Mayo, 2009b). First, as noted in Chapter 3, teacher professional development is essential for effective use of games, and companies are beginning to address this barrier by providing professional development in a variety of online and in-person formats. In addition, there may be barriers to installation and use of third-party software on school systems' computer networks. For example, playing the game should not require video cards, because most student and school administrative office computers have either low-grade video cards or none at all. Similarly, the game should require only modest amounts of random access memory (RAM). Because delivering games on the Internet helps to address these barriers, several experts believe that this approach is promising for scaling up educational games. However, access to the Internet from classroom computers may be constrained by limited bandwidth. In addition, the lack of a computer for each student in many schools limits the potential of games to support individualized learning.

Acceptance of educational games in schools may also be constrained by time and organizational limits. One response to these barriers is to design games that present educational content in short time increments of no more than 40 minutes (the typical class period). Some games present content in less than 10 minutes, allowing the teacher to flexibly integrate them into daily lesson plans. However, in this approach, students have no opportunity for the kinds of extended game play in which they may engage with recreational games—the very kinds of extended game play that have great potential to enhance science learning.

Concerns about protecting individual privacy can also pose a barrier if the game software requests self-identifying information. One solution is to avoid designing such requests into the software, and another is to involve the teacher in entering student contact information and storing it securely. Although delivering games on the Internet can reduce technology hurdles, it also raises privacy and security concerns. These concerns have been addressed in a variety of ways, including placing the game on a dedicated server that only students and teachers can access, preventing navigation to sites other than those related to the game, running background checks on all adults requesting access before allowing them to enter the students' virtual space, and using other types of controls.

Finally, funding limits represent another barrier to increased use of educational games in schools. Inadequate funding can limit the ability of state or school district technology coordinators to purchase site licenses for games, to update computer hardware and software, to enhance Internet access in classrooms, or to provide teacher professional development. This barrier has become more significant, as the current economic downturn has resulted in major cuts to state and local education budgets.

All of these barriers to greater uptake of games in K-12 education, including the primary barrier of a lack of distribution networks, are in various stages of being addressed. Nevertheless, these barriers greatly limit the use of games. In 2009, educational game companies reported having sold only about 200-300 school site licenses for each game, reaching less than 1 percent of the 99,000 public schools in the United States.

Marketing Barriers in Higher Education

Markets for educational games in higher education have more in common with general consumer markets than with K-12 markets. In higher education, as among the general public, an individual can make a final purchasing decision. A professor has greater freedom than a schoolteacher to dictate what textbooks, games, or other curriculum materials will be used in the course and to direct the campus bookstore to buy these materials. The barriers to increased use of games in schools—such as short time segments, state education standards, and technological constraints—are much smaller in higher education. Nevertheless, science learning with games remains rare in college and university classrooms. The exceptions tend to be classes taught by the professors who are also developers of educational games.

Marketing Games to the Public

The general consumer market is much larger than the K-12 and higher education markets, and distribution is much easier, as shown by sales figures for games that have been sold in both markets. For example, Software Kids has sold site licenses for *Time Engineers* to about 300 schools. However, when the company bundled the game with other software in a "Middle School Success" packet offered to the public through stores, it sold 80,000 units. Likewise, Muzzy Lane Software has sold site licenses for *Making History* to only about 250 schools, but was able to sell 40,000-50,000 copies of the consumer version when selling directly to the public.

Parents are the primary purchasers of educational software aimed at younger children, and, as shown by the sales figures above, they continue to play a role in purchases of games targeted to middle school. Parents constitute an important initial target market for scaling up the use of games for science learning. Parent interest in games—expressed through game purchases, observing their children at play, and playing the games with their children—could both increase science learning in the informal context of the home and also encourage greater use of these games in schools. However, parents seeking to advance their children's educational success may want to know more about the effectiveness of a particular game or simulation in supporting science learning before purchasing it. Mayo (2009a, p. 81) observes that "the ability to distinguish between a high- and low-quality product will be essential to the growth and credibility of game-based learning as a field."

By late elementary school, children increasingly make their own decisions about what games to purchase (see Chapter 4). One way to overcome the problem that middle and high school students may avoid a "brainy" game is to sell the game through hardware that is typically purchased by parents. For example, Numedeon partnered with Dell to include *Whyville*, preinstalled on all Dell computers sold at Walmart. Often, the hardware company provides the game developer with a modest payment for each computer (or other hardware unit) sold, which can add up quickly. The game developer can later sell upgrades and add-ons to those hardware purchasers who become interested in the game. Another way to address this problem is through corporate sponsorship, with advertisements and placement of brands within games. In this approach, the corporate sponsor provides some immediate revenue to the developer of an educational game even if sales to preteens and adolescents are slow; it could buy time to implement other marketing strategies to reach this group.

Adults make up a large segment of the general public market, potentially providing a source of sustainable revenue to developers of educational games (Mayo, 2009b). For example, many adult history and strategy buffs have purchased *Making History*. As noted in Chapter 1, *WolfQuest* has attracted adults as well as young people. Adult players of Nintendo DS, a popular handheld gaming device, often purchase educational and self-improvement software; adult gamers comprise one of the fastest growing market segments for Nintendo.

Distribution of games to the general public is facilitated by the presence of "turnkey publishers," who will carry out all manufacturing and marketing-related tasks, such as packaging, obtaining a rating from the Entertainment Software Rating Board, advertising, bundling with related products, and negotiating sales agreements with retail outlets. However, the game developer who uses this distribution channel loses both control of the product and a share of the profits to the publisher. A game developer may also hire a distributor, which does no marketing or advertising but can inject the game into a network of stores with which it has agreements.

The effectiveness of the Internet as a distribution mechanism depends on the website hosting a game. If it is not well known, the game may be invisible to most consumers. However, it may still be possible to increase awareness of a new game by constant, aggressive efforts to submit it to game review sites, game award contests, product review columns, and appropriate social networking sites.

The company executives interviewed by Mayo (2009b) reported few barriers to consumer acceptance among the general public. In fact, they noted that the public's interest in learning generally enhances acceptance of educational games.

Marketing educational games to the public is constrained by far fewer barriers than exist in K-12 education. Distribution is facilitated through publishers and pure distributors, and consumer acceptance is in line with other learning products. All other factors being equal, games designed for science leaning should reach scale first and foremost in the public market. However, few educational games have been actively and professionally marketed to the public, and none has been professionally marketed in higher education. This is due partly to the lack of a commercial-grade product to bring to market, which is related to the lack of funding to support the required final hardening, consumer acceptance testing, and refining. It is also due to academic developers' lack of understanding of the complete life cycle of game development, marketing, and maintenance.

ALTERNATIVE PATHWAYS TO SCALE

The committee identified two overall models for bringing science learning games and simulations to scale: (1) a traditional "top-down" model of sales and distribution of games or simulations and their supporting systems to schools and school districts, and (2) a "disruptive innovation" model (Christensen, Horn, and Johnson, 2008). In the disruptive innovation model, widespread use of simulations and games for informal science learning by individuals and families would demonstrate a dramatic improvement over traditional science education, leading school systems to greatly increase their adoption of simulations and games. Success in this second model, elements of which could be emerging, could prove to be a way to enable wider use of games in the first model.

Within the disruptive innovation model, there are a number of promising pathways toward scaling up the use of simulations and games. One is represented by the growing number of small commercial publishers of educational games. Other pathways include nonprofit organizations taking on more of the roles of game publishers and a decentralized "commons" approach that encourages collaborative development and dissemination of games and simulations. The following section describes these three pathways, followed by a sketch of the possibilities for a traditional, top-down model of scaling up games through school systems.

Small Commercial Publishers

Mayo (2009b) observed that a business model of modest up-front investment in game development followed by long-term returns appears to be working for a new group of small-scale educational game developers, such as Muzzy Lane Software, 360Ed, Tabula Digita, Numedeon, and Software Kids. These companies have sold tens of thousands of copies of educational games. Unlike commercial games, which may be popular for only a few months, academic games should sell for years, as the scientific principles and concepts underlying the game remain unchanged. Although the content of an academic game need not change, the game will require ongoing support to keep pace with changes in its supporting hardware and software.

Nonprofit Organizations as Game Publishers

Gershenfeld (2009) proposed that science learning games could be scaled up if game development funders—foundations, nonprofit organizations, universities, government agencies—took on the roles of commercial game publishers. Publishers are responsible for the entire game life cycle, including marketing, distribution, business development, and ongoing support for the games. Lacking expertise in these areas, funders have invested millions of dollars in educational games that have reached only a handful of players—because they were not fun to play or were not effectively marketed or distributed.

Nonprofits could carry out a rigorous screening process to decide which games to fund and at what level—just as commercial publishers do. When considering a potential game concept, nonprofits would ask such questions as:

- Who is the target audience (e.g., consumer, school system, library) and the purchaser (e.g., child, parent, teacher, department head)?
- What is the desired learning goal or impact (e.g., science learning goals, a role in the core curriculum, a supplement)?
- What evidence is there of market demand? Answering this question may require testing the game concept in target markets.
- What is the best game platform to reach the target audience? This involves considering technology options (alternative video consoles, handheld devices, personal computers, etc.) for the target audience.
- What is the business model? Will the game be sold as a product (e.g., by retail, by download) or as a service (subscription, micropayment, etc.)?
- What are the financial requirements and expectations? This will include considering how best to balance the potential financial and social/educational returns and deciding on an appropriate budget for the project.
- What is the most effective team to develop the game? An understanding of who the audience is, the platforms, and the business models is necessary to select the best development team.
- Is there a well-thought-out development plan with natural funding milestones?
- Who is the most effective team to market the game?
- What is the methodology and plan for assessment? This involves ongoing review of the project and repeated testing with target purchasers to ensure it is on track.
- What is the overall threshold to approve the game project? This includes deciding who is on the "greenlight" committee and carefully defining the necessary milestones and approval process.

Nonprofit organizations will need to develop new knowledge and skills to answer these questions, Gershenfeld (2009) observed, and they will also need to learn from their successes and failures. Creating partnerships with individuals, teams, and organizations can help them to build the needed knowledge and skills. In this pathway, nonprofits would use a similar business model to that of commercial publishers—developing and marketing a few blockbuster science learning games.

A Decentralized Approach

Osterweil (2009) advocates a decentralized pathway to scaling up educational games by building on the burgeoning independent games movement. He notes that a typical commercial game has only a few weeks either to recoup its investment in retail outlets or to find itself consigned to the remainders bin. To achieve this rapid payback, commercial games require very large marketing budgets, which may equal their development costs. Independent games, in contrast, are often distributed online, an environment much more conducive to targeted marketing and niche sales. Because of their small size, they can be created in a fraction of the time and cost required for a large commercial game. Many different groups and individuals, including students and industry professionals working in their spare time, are creating a variety of independent games, some of high quality. These developments contrast with the current, centralized approach to developing games for science learning, in which foundations and other funders have invested heavily in a few academics and small firms, who in turn produce a few large educational games.

The current trend toward web-based delivery of games would facilitate this decentralized pathway to scale for several reasons. First, web delivery is more effective for reaching small, niche markets. It allows consumers to download free demonstrations or make incremental purchases, a form of marketing that favors the independent developer without a large advertising budget to build demand. Second, web-delivered games can reach K-12 students and schools, overcoming some of the hardware and software barriers described above. Third, languages for creating web-delivered games are becoming increasingly sophisticated; some such languages can be used to create more than flat, simple two-dimensional games. A web-based market for science learning games could serve as a laboratory for diverse approaches, allowing best practices to emerge, rather than be preordained by a few experts.

Osterweil suggests that funders could create market conditions that would facilitate this decentralized pathway by supporting the creation of shared web platforms for development and distribution of educational games. Current examples of such platforms—the iPhone app store and the Android market—provide models for creating a new platform specifically to support science learning games. Each has inspired creative development of myriad applications by providing an easy development platform and lowering barriers to entering the marketplace. Another example is BrainPOP, a privately held company that has created a site with videos on a wide range of school topics, indexed by grade and subject area and keyed to state educational standards for easy use by teachers. Thousands of schools have purchased annual subscriptions to access these materials.

A Top-Down Pathway to Scale

Zelman (2009) suggests that top-down educational policies can facilitate widespread adoption of simulations and games for science learning, overcoming the marketing barriers in K-12 education discussed above. She describes public education as a system, with classroom instruction at the center. Four related elements affect classroom instruction: (1) local, state, and federal accountability policies; (2) student, family, and community support; (3) educator professional development; and (4) state fiscal policies and educational technology plans.

Current developments throughout this system present new opportunities for scaling up the use of games and simulations for science learning. At the national level, states are joining to develop common core educational standards, including science standards that are expected to be higher, clearer, and fewer than current science standards. At the same time, the U.S. Department of Education is supporting consortia of states in developing shared assessments. These new standards and assessments may incorporate the broad range of science learning goals that games and simulations are well suited to advance.

Zelman argues that states and school districts are becoming more interested in technology as one route to improving the effectiveness of instruction and enhancing student performance on assessments. To foster this interest, the U.S. Department of Education (2010) recently published a draft National Education Technology Plan outlining local, state, and federal technology policies in the areas of learning, assessment, teaching, infrastructure, and productivity. Since 2002, the Department has provided grants to states to assist them in purchasing learning technology. As part of the grants program, the states are required to create educational technology development plans.

Zelman (2009) identified several state policies that might encourage wider use of simulations and games, including revising curriculum purchasing procedures that currently focus on textbooks to facilitate statewide software and hardware purchases. She advocates focusing state educational technology plans on the goals of ensuring statewide availability of computer hardware and software and broadband access, eliminating firewalls while maintaining security, and assisting in the distribution and marketing of educational games. She argues that such policies would increase science learning, not only at school, but also through family gaming at home. Such technology policies would also facilitate the development of common educational data standards across the 50 states, making statewide performance data highly accessible, including for teachers, along with digital learning objects and online mentoring and professional development.

At the level of the individual school, Zelman suggests designating some schools as gaming schools and laboratories. At these schools, data would be gathered to evaluate the effectiveness of games in helping students achieve educational standards and the types of assessment data that can be gained from games. Other topics that could be explored in these schools include identifying the types of knowledge teachers require to use games effectively to support science learning; the financial costs of hardware, software, and teacher training, and how to budget for these costs; the roles of games in supporting informal learning after school, at home, and with peers; and the potential for collaborating with public radio and television stations.

CONCLUSIONS

Increasing the uptake of games for science learning is affected by a variety of barriers. Some of these barriers slow development and sales of games in both formal and informal learning contexts, while others are unique to the formal contexts of K-12 and higher education.

Conclusion: *Several barriers slow large-scale development and use of games and simulations for science learning in K-12 and higher education. There is not yet a coherent market for either games or simulations in schools that is analogous to the textbook market. Increased use of games and simulations in schools and universities will require clear alignment with curriculum and professional development support for teachers or faculty members. These issues are dealt with primarily at the local level in highly decentralized structures, posing a serious barrier to scaling up the use of games and simulations. If districts, schools, and universities express interest, this will encourage the development and use of these new learning technologies.*

The committee identified two basic models for scaling up the use of games and simulations for science learning.

Conclusion: *There appear to be two basic possible models for reaching scale: (1) a traditional top-down model of sales and distribution of games or simulations and their supporting systems to schools and school districts and (2) a model of sales and distribution to parents, students, and individuals for informal learning. Success in the second model, elements of which could be emerging, could prove to be a way to enable access to the first model.*

The committee explored alternative pathways for reaching scale. Pathways within the second model include the small commercial game or simulation publisher, the "nonprofit" publisher with foundation or government agency funding, and a decentralized approach that would support collaborative game development and distribution. A few small commercial publishers have successfully marketed educational games to parents and children. Parents could potentially constitute a large market for increased sales of games and simulations designed for science learning.

Conclusion: *Parents of K-6 students concerned about their children's educational progress could constitute a large and important initial market for increased sales and use of science learning simulations and games. However, parents may have questions about the educational value of various simulations and games, and these questions could potentially be addressed through the creation of a respected, independent, third-party system to evaluate and certify educational effectiveness.*

The availability and quality of computer hardware and software systems greatly influence the extent to which individuals access and use simulations and games for science learning, in both formal and informal learning environments. Computer technology continues to change rapidly, requiring ongoing support for simulations and games.

Conclusion: *Simulations and games for science learning require a sustained approach. Because a game or simulation needs to be updated and improved on an ongoing basis, it is not enough to simply develop and launch a stand-alone game or simulation. An ongoing development, research, and support effort is required for dissemination at scale.*

A large number of stakeholders—including commercial entertainment companies, academic researchers, state and local education officials, game developers, and teachers—play a role in the use of simulations and games for science learning. Bringing these stakeholders together in partnerships could help bring research and development of simulations to scale.

Conclusion: *Partnerships that include industry developers, academic researchers, designers, learning scientists, and educational practitioners could play an important role in scaling up research and development of games and simulations.*

7

Research Agenda for Simulations and Games

The weak science achievement of U.S. elementary and secondary students reflects the uneven quality of current science education. Although young children come to school with innate curiosity and intuitive ideas about the world around them, science classes rarely foster their interest. Students spend time reading science texts, listening to lectures, carrying out preordained "cookbook" laboratory activities, and memorizing the disparate science facts that are emphasized in high-stakes science tests, increasingly losing interest in science as they move from elementary school to middle and high school.

Many experts call for a new approach to science education, based on a growing body of cognitive research indicating that science learning is a multifaceted process involving much more than recall of facts (National Research Council, 2005b, 2007, 2009). In this approach, teachers and instructional materials spark students' interest by engaging them in exploration of natural phenomena and support their learning with several forms of instruction. Students simultaneously develop conceptual understanding of these phenomena and science process skills while maintaining their motivation for continued science learning. The new approach reflects growing understanding of the critical importance of interest and enthusiasm in scaffolding science learning.

Computer simulations and games have great potential to catalyze and support the new approach, by allowing learners to explore natural phenomena that they cannot directly observe, due to time scale (too fast or slow), size (too big or small), or form (e.g., radio waves). Learners can manipulate virtual systems that represent these natural phenomena, a process that helps them to draw powerful mental connections between the representations and the phenomena and to formulate scientifically correct explanations for the phenomena.

Overall, the evidentiary base for learning science from simulations is stronger than that for games. There is promising evidence that simulations enhance conceptual science learning and moderate evidence that they increase students' motivation for science learning. Emerging evidence from a small number of examples suggests that well-designed games can motivate students, encourage them to identify with science and science learning, and enhance conceptual understanding—but overall the research on games remains inconclusive.

Although both simulations and games have been used for training and education for over three decades, their effectiveness for science learning has not been studied broadly or systematically. Reaching the potential of simulations and games to motivate and engage science students, enhance science achievement, and advance other science learning goals will require a stronger, more systematic approach to research and development.

The committee's proposed research agenda outlines such an approach. The first section of the agenda focuses on improving the overall quality of the research, the second section outlines particular topics requiring further study, and the third section identifies approaches to institutionalizing research and development on games and simulations for science learning.

Improving Research Quality

Research on how simulations and games support science learning has not kept pace with the rapid development of these new learning technologies. Although the evidence base related to simulations is stronger than that related to games, both areas are thin. Much research has been exploratory, making it difficult to generalize, because researchers and developers have not always clearly defined the desired learning outcomes or the mechanisms by which the simulation or game is expected to advance these outcomes.

The committee recommends that future research on simulations and games follow a design-based approach aimed at continuous improvement, including the following steps:

- *Researchers and developers should clearly specify the desired learning outcomes of a simulation or game and describe in detail how it is expected to advance these outcomes. This should include description of the design features that are hypothesized to activate learning, the intended use of these design features, and the underlying learning theory. Researchers should also indicate direct evidence of student learning, if such evidence is available. This will allow research findings to accumulate, providing a base for improved designs to further enhance the effectiveness of games and simulations for learning.*

- *Researchers should initially develop methodologies for both the design and evaluation of games and simulations that focus on continual improvement. The use of such methodologies will help to ensure that large studies are not outdated by the time they are published, due to changes in technology and advances in cognitive science.*
- *Researchers should consider collaborating on "model games." Such games would enable controlled research studies in which investigators develop variations on the models and test them among different groups of learners to address a suite of related research questions about factors that may influence the effectiveness of games as learning tools. New model games would build iteratively on old models, based on this research.*

Filling Gaps in the Research

The Role of Simulations and Games in Learning

Studies of the effectiveness of simulations and games for science learning have tended to focus on assessing conceptual understanding alone. The research has given little attention to the broader science learning goals advocated by science education experts. Research is needed to improve understanding of how simulations and games can best motivate learners, engage them in active investigations, and build understanding of science processes as well as concepts.

- *Researchers should assess the potential of games and simulations to advance a broad set of science learning goals, including motivation, conceptual understanding, science process skills, understanding of the nature of science, scientific discourse, and identification with science and science learning. Such research is needed to more clearly illuminate the full range of science competencies that can be supported with simulations and games.*

This report has shown that simulations and games have potential to address critical weaknesses in current science education by meeting the individual learning needs of both low-achieving and advanced science students, embedding science learning in the context of engaging real-world problems, and improving access to high-quality science learning experiences in formal and informal settings. An important first step toward reaching this potential is to increase basic understanding of the processes of learning when individuals interact with simulations and games.

Research on the Learning Process

- *Research should examine the mediating processes within the individual that influence science learning with simulations and games. This research would aim to illuminate what happens within the individual—both emotionally and cognitively—that leads to learning and what design features appear to activate these responses. For example, a game may arouse an emotional response and/or encourage the learner to set goals. Over time, such studies might begin to identify the ways in which different design features activate shared emotional and cognitive responses that support science learning across individuals.*

- *Research on games should seek to develop empirical links between different types of motivators and different learning outcomes. For example, extrinsic motivators, such as points or opportunities to advance to a higher level of game play, may encourage learners to repeat and remember important science or mathematics facts, while intrinsic motivators, such as satisfying one's own curiosity or interest, may motivate deeper conceptual understanding and development of science process skills. Social motivators, such as the desire to participate or to establish an identity in a group of game players, might be particularly effective in encouraging the development of scientific discourse and identification with science and science learning.*

- *Research should examine the role of metacognition and awareness of oneself as a learner when an individual interacts with a simulation or game. Prior research on science learning suggests that making learning goals explicit and supporting learners in metacognition— reflecting on their own learning—enhance learning. In contrast, simulations and games can be designed to support "accidental" learning through playful engagement. Research is needed to determine whether, and to what extent, science learning may take place even if the learner is not aware that he or she is engaged in learning.*

- *Studies are needed to explore which individuals and groups prefer which types of simulations and games for science learning, as well as the durability of such preferences. They should consider how individual preferences are related to individual personality traits, broader group characteristics, the nature of the learning experience itself, learning processes, and learning goals. These studies should also consider how context and experience can broaden or change individual and group preferences.*

- *Researchers should establish stronger theoretical underpinnings for the use of simulations and games by connecting research on simulations and games to the relevant theory and research on learning more generally, drawing on social and cognitive psychology, human-computer interactions, anthropology, and other fields that study learning.*

Contextualizing Learning and Learning Transfer

Although simulations and games provide contexts that can motivate and support learning, research on games has shown that learners may focus on the context or narrative to an extent that slows development of a deeper understanding of science concepts. Research is needed to explore this tension and illuminate how best to create virtual contexts that both motivate learners and support durable, transferable learning.

- *Studies should examine how learning contexts created in simulations and games may advance or hinder attainment of different science learning goals. For example, engaging students in the context of a virtual investigation of a real-life problem may simultaneously advance multiple learning goals (e.g., conceptual learning and science process skills), or it may advance one or more goals while having no effect on slowing attainment of others.*
- *Future studies should examine transfer of learning from the simulation or game learning environment to other contexts. These studies should examine how transfer occurs (including the features of simulations and games that support transfer), the extent of transfer, and whether including data drawn directly from the real world in simulations and games influences students' understanding of science processes and/or motivates them to make real-world decisions based on evidence.*
- *Research is needed to examine the durability of science learning that is advanced through interaction with simulations and games. For example, some individuals develop feelings of identity with science and science learning through extended interactions with games. Investigators should track such individuals over several years to assess the extent to which this identification with science translates into sustained science achievement. In addition, they should conduct retrospective studies to assess the extent to which identity with science developed through gaming may encourage entry into science careers.*

Increasing Access to High-Quality Learning Experiences

Overcoming current barriers to the use of simulations and games to help all students learn science requires research and development in a number of areas. This section of the research agenda focuses on research related to learning; in later sections, the committee recommends research to understand and mitigate constraints to wider use of simulations and games.

- *Future research should investigate how simulations and games can support diverse learners in science and mitigate particular individual or group learning difficulties, such as lower science achievement levels, limited English proficiency, lower general cognitive ability, learning disabilities, or attention deficit hyperactivity disorder.*
- *Research should examine whether, and to what extent, diverse learners develop intuitive understandings of science processes and scientific modeling through play in the model-based virtual worlds of recreational games and how games designed for science learning can build on these intuitive understandings to develop knowledge of science processes and the nature of science.*

Using Simulations and Games in Formal and Informal Contexts

Simulations and games have potential to enhance science learning in formal contexts, such as science classrooms or online science courses, and in informal contexts, such as homes, after-school clubs, libraries, and recreation or science centers. Research to date has shown that the context significantly shapes how learners interact with a simulation or game and the extent to which this interaction supports science learning. Further research is needed to more fully understand how different contexts affect learning with simulations and games and to investigate how the design of learning environments might impact learning. To supplement the research recommended above, which would use model games to assess the influence of different contexts, researchers should

- *Investigate how best to integrate games into formal learning contexts (K-12 and higher education) and informal learning contexts (e.g., home, science museum, after-school club) to enhance learning. This should include studies of how internal scaffolds in the simulation or game and external scaffolds provided by a teacher, mentor, peers, or other instructional resources (either in person or via various online mechanisms) support science learning in different contexts.*
- *Examine current policy and practice barriers that slow the adoption and use of high-quality simulations and games for science learning in K-12 and higher education. This research should include examination of such barriers as the need for teacher and faculty professional development and the limited availability and quality of assessments; technological barriers, and barriers to research in real-world settings.*

Studies of barriers in K-12 education should examine the role of current state science standards and accountability systems as barriers to increased use of simulations and games.

* *Examine social and cultural factors in both formal and informal learning contexts that influence how widely simulations and games are used for science learning. Investigators should examine how children and adolescents, parents, caregivers, informal educators, teachers, school administrators, and education officials perceive the educational and entertainment value of games and how these perceptions may enhance or limit wider use of games designed for science learning. The findings of this research should be used to develop targeted solutions that should then be tested for effectiveness in intervention research.*

* *Examine the potential of different types of simulations and games, as well as different types of delivery platforms, to bridge informal and formal science learning. This should include research on the potential of "lightweight" games that can be easily accessed on the web using cell phones and other mobile devices to support learning across boundaries of time and space.*

* *Study the potential of structured informal learning environments, such as after-school clubs and online learning communities, as promising contexts for science learning with simulations and games. Such studies should examine how learning in these environments may transfer to or support further science learning in the classroom and at home.*

* *Study how engaging learners in implementing or modifying existing science learning games or designing new science learning games may advance one or more science learning goals.*

Assessing and Supporting Individualized Learning

Research on how to effectively assess student learning with simulations and games and use that information to impact the learning process is still in its infancy, although initial work seems promising. Achieving the potential of simulations and games for assessment and learning will require research and development in all areas of assessment: development, implementation, and evaluation. In particular, research is needed on:

* *Applications of the evidence-centered design approach to the development of assessments of learning through simulations and games. Developers and testing experts should collaborate to clearly identify desired learning goals and the kinds of evidence needed to show learner progress toward these goals; they should use these specifica-*

tions to design tasks and test items in ways that will provide the needed evidence. Modeling of the motivation and thinking of the learner will need to evolve simultaneously with the "physical" modeling of the game or simulation.

- *The development and use of flexible statistical models and machine learning to make meaning from the large amounts of data provided by simulations and games. These measurement methods are well suited to application in simulations and games, because they can handle uncertainty about the current state of the learner, provide immediate feedback during tasks, and model complex patterns of student behavior and multiple forms of evidence. Continued research on these methods will help to improve assessment in simulations and games.*

Assessment tasks seamlessly embedded into game play and linked to instructional supports have great potential to support individualized science learning. Simulations and games can be designed to rapidly interpret learner performance on these tasks, using the information to provide the learner (and teacher) with feedback, coaching, or new information or learning challenges, based on the student's unique capabilities and learning needs. These promising developments, if supported by further research, could lead to radical improvements in self-directed science learning and the authentic assessment of science learning.

- *Researchers should continue to advance the design and use of techniques that (1) rapidly measure and adapt to students' progress in a specific learning progression, (2) dynamically respond to an individual student's performance, and (3) allow for the summative evaluation of how well students are learning.*

Scaling Up Simulations and Games

The committee identified two possible models for reaching scale in the use of simulations and games for science learning in formal education: (1) a traditional top-down market model, in which games or simulations are sold or distributed to universities, schools, and school districts, and (2) a market model in which widespread use of simulations and games for informal science learning by parents, students, and individuals could dramatically change how science is learned and taught in schools and colleges. Neither model can become reality without research to more clearly illuminate the current barriers to implementation and to identify approaches to overcoming these barriers. For example, there is not yet a coherent market for either games or simulations in schools that is analogous to the textbook market, and the bewildering variety of games and simulations for science learning available for free or for purchase can leave potential customers confused. The committee recommends the following:

- *Research to better understand key factors that will enable both the education marketplace and the informal learning marketplace to embrace games and simulations for science learning. The goals of this research should be to increase understanding of key design features that enhance the appeal and uptake of games and simulations and market forces that affect adoption across formal and informal learning contexts.*
- *Research and development partnerships should be established to investigate alternative mechanisms for supporting large-scale collaborative innovation in science education based on the use of simulations and games and to support ongoing improvement in simulations and games.*
- *Research on the feasibility of systems for informing users or consumers about the quality and educational effectiveness of simulations and games designed for science learning, such as expert rating systems. This research should explore the potential of such systems to serve as catalysts for distribution of high-quality simulations and games.*

Institutionalizing Research and Development

To carry out all elements of this research agenda, the committee recommends creating research and development partnerships:

- *Academic researchers, developers and entrepreneurs from the gaming industry, and education practitioners and policy makers should form research and development partnerships to facilitate rich intellectual collaboration. These partnerships, which may be large or small, should coordinate and share information internally and with other partnerships and should*
  —*share resources and tools, thereby reducing costs and allowing reusability;*
  —*provide researchers with shared points of access to students and their educational records and to informal learners, at the same time conducting research that assists formal and informal learning institutions;*
  —*explore alternative approaches to—and economic models for— extending the life cycle of simulations and games with ongoing updating and maintenance; and*

—investigate how to optimize educational contexts for simulations and games—including alternative technologies and platforms, teacher preparation and professional development, and curricular supports—for different populations of K-12 and adult learners.

- *Government agencies and foundations may consider the potential benefits of providing sustained support for such partnerships.*
- *Government agencies and foundations may consider the potential benefits of funding research and development of new models for delivering learning opportunities through simulations and games that can be self-sustaining and reach a broad audience.*
- *Researchers in the software and gaming industries, government agencies, and academic institutions should continue their research and development of new, open-source authoring tools to facilitate development of games and simulations.*

The research agenda outlined in this chapter is meant to provide guidance to active and prospective researchers, simulation and game developers, commercial publishers, and funders. However, games and simulations designed for science learning are played and used by a wide variety of individuals in rapidly changing markets. In the future, this research agenda may change with advances in technology, shifts in consumer preferences, and changes in the education environment. The committee expects that, if implemented, the research agenda will have to adapt and evolve in tandem with the evolution of the field of educational simulations and games.

References and Bibliography

Adams, W.K., Reid, S., LeMaster, R., McKagan, S.B., Perkins, K.K., Dubson, M., and Wieman. C.E. (2008a). A study of educational simulations part I—Engagement and learning. *Journal of Interactive Learning Research, 19*(3), 397-419.

Adams, W.K., Reid, S., LeMaster, R., McKagan, S.B., Perkins, K.K., Dubson, M., and Wieman, C.E. (2008b). A study of educational simulations part II—Interface design. *Journal of Interactive Learning Research, 19*(4), 551-577.

Anderson, J., and Barnett, G.M. (in press). Using video games to support pre-service elementary teachers learning of basic physics principles. *Journal of Science Education and Technology.*

Annetta, L., Minogue, J., Holmes, S.Y., and Cheng, M.-T. (2009). Investigating the impact of videogames on high school students' engagement and learning about genetics. *Computers and Education, 53*(1), 74-85.

Baker, E.L., and Delacruz, G.C. (2008). A framework for the assessment of learning games. In H.F. O'Neil and R.S. Perez (Eds.), *Computer games and team and individual learning* (pp. 21-37). Oxford, UK: Elsevier.

Baker, E.L., and Mayer, R.E. (1999). Computer-based assessment of problem solving. *Computers in Human Behavior, 15,* 269-282.

Banilower, E., Cohen, K., Pasley, J., and Weiss, I. (2008). *Effective science instruction: What does research tell us?* Portsmouth, NH: RMC Research Corporation, Center on Instruction. Available: http://www.centeroninstruction.org/files/Characteristics%20of%20Effective%20Science%20Instruction%20REVISED%20FINAL.pdf [accessed April 19, 2010].

Barab, S.A. (2009). *The Quest Atlantis project: A 21st century curriculum.* Paper commissioned for the National Research Council Workshop on Gaming and Simulations, October 6-7, Washington, DC. Available: http://www7.nationalacademies.org/bose/Gaming_Sims_Commissioned_Papers.html [accessed March 16, 2010].

Barab, S.A., and Dede, C. (2007). Games and immersive participatory simulations for science education: An emerging type of curricula. *Journal of Science Education and Technology, 16*(1), 1-3.

Barab, S.A., Arici, A., and Jackson, C. (2005). Eat your vegetables and do your homework: A design based investigation of enjoyment and meaning in learning. *Educational Technology, 45*(1), 15-20.

Barab, S.A., Sadler, T.D., Heiselt, C., Hickey, D., and Zuiker, S. (2007). Relating narrative, inquiry, and inscriptions: Supporting consequential play. *Journal of Science Education and Technology, 16*(1), 59-82.

Barman, C.R. (1999). Students' views about scientists and school science: Engaging K-8 teachers in a national study. *Journal of Science Teacher Education, 10*(1), 43-54.

Barnett, M., Squire, K., Higginbotham, T., and Grant, J. (2004). Electromagnetism supercharged! In *Proceedings of the 2004 International Conference of the Learning Sciences.* Los Angeles: University of California Press.

Barron, B. (2006). Interest and self-sustained learning as catalysts of development: A learning ecology perspective. *Human Development, 49*(4), 153-224.

Baxter, G.P., Shavelson, R., Goldman, S.R., and Pine, J. (1992). Evaluation of procedure-based scoring for hands-on science assessment. *Journal of Educational Measurement, 29*(1), 1-17.

Beck, I.L., McKeown, M.G., and Kucan, L. (2002). *Bringing words to life: Robust vocabulary instruction.* New York: Guilford Press.

Behrens, J.T. (2009). *Response to assessment of student learning in science simulations and games.* Paper prepared for the National Research Council Workshop on Gaming and Simulations. Available: http://www7.nationalacademies.org/bose/Behrens_Gaming_CommissionedPaper.pdf [accessed March 23, 2010].

Behrens, J.T., Frezzo, D.C., Mislevy, R.J., Kroopnick, M., and Wise, D. (2008). Structural, Functional, and Semiotic Symmetries in Simulation-Based Games and Assessments. In E. Baker, J. Dickieson, W. Wulfeck, and H.F. O'Neill (Eds.), *Assessment of problem solving using simulations* (pp. 59-80). New York: Routledge.

Bennett, R.E., Persky, H., Wiss, A. and Jenkins, F. (2007). *Problem solving in technology rich environments: A report from the NAEP technology-based assessment project.* NCES 2007-466. Washington, DC: U.S. Department of Education, National Center for Education Statistics. Available: http://nces.ed.gov/pubsearch/pubsinfo.asp?pubid=2007466 [accessed July 28, 2010].

Bewley, W., Chung, G., Delacruz, G., and Baker, E. (2009). Assessment models and tools for virtual environment training. In D. Schmorrow, J. Cohn, and D. Nicholson (Eds.), *The PSI handbook of virtual environments for training and education: Developments for the military and beyond, volume 1* (pp. 300-313). Westport, CT: Greenwood.

Bishop, C.M. (2006). *Pattern recognition and machine learning.* New York: Springer.

Bloom, B.S. (1956). *Taxonomy of educational objectives. Handbook 1: Cognitive domain.* New York: David McKay.

Blosser, P.E. (1990). *Procedures to increase the entry of women in science-related careers.* (ERIC/ SMEAC Science Education Digest No. 1; ERIC Identifier ED321977). Columbus OH: ERIC Clearinghouse for Science Mathematics and Environmental Education.

Bransford, J.D., and Schwartz, D.L. (1999). Rethinking transfer: A simple proposal with multiple implications. *Review of Research in Education, 24,* 61-100.

Brown, J., Hinze, S., and Pellegrino, J.W. (2008). Technology and formative assessment. In T. Good (Ed.), *21st century education*. Thousand Oaks, CA: Sage.

Brown, L. (1992). The new world order. In A.K. Tripathi and V.B. Bhatt (Eds.), *Changing environmental ideologies* (pp.19-35). New Delhi: Ashish.

Bruckman, A., Jensen, C., and DeBonte, A. (2002). *Gender and programming achievement in a CSCL environment*. Paper prepared for the Conference on Computer-Supported Collaborative Learning, Boulder, CO.

Bryk, A.S., and Raudenbush, S.W. (1992). *Hierarchical linear models: Applications and data analysis methods*. Newbury Park, CA: Sage.

Buckingham, D. (2007). *Beyond technology: Children's learning in the age of digital culture*. Malden, MA: Polity Press.

Buckingham, D., and Scanlon, M. (2002). *Education, entertainment and learning in the home*. London: Open University Press.

Buckley, B.C., Gobert, J.D., and Horwitz, P. (2006). Using log files to track students' model-based inquiry. *Proceedings of the 7th International Conference on the Learning Sciences*. Bloomington, IN: International Society of the Learning Sciences.

Buckley, B.C., Gobert, J., Horwitz, P., and O'Dwyer, L. (2009). Looking inside the black box: Assessing model-based learning and inquiry in BioLogica. *International Journal of Learning Technology, 5*(2), 166-190.

Cavallo, A.M., and Laubach, T.A. (2001). Students' science perceptions and enrollment decisions in differing learning cycle classrooms. *Journal of Research in Science Teaching, 38*(9), 1,029-1,062.

Chang, H.-Y. (2009). Use of critique to enhance learning with an interactive molecular visualization of thermal conductivity. In M.D. Linn (Chair), *Critique to learning science*. Symposium conducted at the annual meeting of the National Association for Research in Science Teaching, Garden Grove, CA.

Chase, C., Chin, D.B., Oppezzo, M., and Schwartz, D.L. (2009). Teachable agents and the protégé effect: Increasing the effort towards learning. *Journal of Science Education and Technology, 18*(4).

Christensen, C.M., Horn, M.B., and Johnson, C.W. (2008). *Disrupting class: How disruptive innovation will change the way the world learns*. Chicago: McGraw-Hill.

Clark, C., and Mayer, R. (2003). *E-Learning and the science of instruction*. San Francisco: Pfeiffer.

Clark, D.B. (2006). Longitudinal conceptual change in students' understanding of thermal equilibrium: An examination of the process of conceptual restructuring. *Cognition and Instruction, 24*(4), 467-563.

Clark, D.B., and Jorde, D. (2004). Helping students revise disruptive experientially-supported ideas about thermodynamics: Computer visualizations and tactile models. *Journal of Research in Science Teaching, 41*(1), 1-23.

Clark, D.B., and Linn, M.C. (2003). Scaffolding knowledge integration through curricular depth. *Journal of Learning Sciences, 12*(4), 451-494.

Clark, D.B., and Sampson, V.D. (2005, June). *Analyzing the quality of argumentation supported by personally-seeded discussions*. Paper presented at the annual meeting of the Conference on Computer-Supported Collaborative Learning, Taipei, Taiwan.

Clark, D.B., and Sampson, V.D. (2006, July). Evaluating argumentation in science: New assessment tools. *Proceedings of the 7th International Conference on the Learning Sciences*. Bloomington, IN: International Society of the Learning Sciences.

Clark, D.B., and Sampson, V.D. (2007). Personally-seeded discussions to scaffold online argumentation. *International Journal of Science Education, 29*(3), 253-277.

Clark, D.B., and Sampson, V.D. (2008). Assessing dialogic argumentation in online environments to relate structure, grounds, and conceptual quality. *Journal of Research in Science Teaching, 45*(3), 6.

Clark, D.B., Nelson, B., Sengupta, P., and D'Angelo, C. (2009). *Rethinking science learning through digital games and simulations: Genres, examples, and evidence*. Paper commissioned for the National Research Council Workshop on Gaming and Simulations, October 6-7, Washington, DC. Available: http://www7.nationalacademies.org/bose/Gaming_Sims_Commissioned_Papers.html [accessed March 23, 2010].

Clark, D.B., Nelson, B., D'Angelo, C.M., Slack, K., and Menekse, M. (2010). *Connecting students' intuitive understandings about kinematics and Newtonian mechanics into explicit formalized frameworks*. Paper presented at the American Association for the Advancement of Science (AAAS) Conference, San Diego.

Clarke, J., and Dede, C. (2005). *Making learning meaningful: An exploratory study of using multi-user environments (MUVEs) in middle school science*. Paper prepared for the American Educational Research Association Conference, April, Montreal, Quebec.

Clarke, J., and Dede, C. (2009). Robust designs for scalability. In L. Moller, J.B. Huett, and D.M. Harvey (Eds.), *Learning and instructional technologies for the 21st century: Visions of the future* (pp. 27-48). New York: Springer.

Cognition and Technology Group at Vanderbilt. (1990). Anchored instruction and its relationship to situated cognition. *Educational Researcher, 19*, 2-10.

Cohen-Scali, V. (2003). The influence of family, social, and work socialization on the construction of the professional identity of young adults. *Journal of Career Development, 29*(4), 237-249.

Colella, V. (2000). Participatory simulations: Building collaborative understanding through immersive dynamic modeling. *Journal of the Learning Sciences, 9*(4), 471-500.

Collins, A., and Halverson, R. (2009). *Rethinking education in the age of technology*. New York: Teachers College Press.

Colzato, L.S., van Leeuwen, P.J.A., van den Wildenberg, W.P.M., and Hommel, B. (2010). DOOM'd to switch: Superior cognitive flexibility in players of first-person shooter games. *Frontiers in Psychology, 1*, 1-5.

Cooper, M.M., and Stevens, R. (2008). Reliable multi-method assessment of metacognition use in chemistry problem solving. *Chemistry Education Research and Practice, 9*, 18-24.

Crowley, K., and Jacobs, M. (2002). Islands of expertise and the development of family scientific literacy. In G. Leinhardt, K. Crowley, and K. Knutson (Eds.), *Learning conversations in museums*. Mahwah, NJ: Lawrence Erlbaum.

Cuadros, J., and Yaron, D. (2007). "One firm spot": The role of homework as a lever in acquiring conceptual and performance competence in college chemistry. *Journal of Chemical Education, 84*(6), 1,047-1,052.

Culp, K.M. (2009). *Response to: Learning context: Gaming, simulations, and science learning in the classroom*. Paper commissioned for the National Research Council Workshop on Gaming and Simulations, October 6-7, Washington, DC. Available: http://www7.nationalacademies.org/bose/Culp_Gaming_Presentation. pdf [accessed March 23, 2010].

Day, S.B., and Goldstone, R.L. (2009). Analogical transfer from interaction with a simulated physical system. In *Proceedings of the Thirty-First Annual Conference of the Cognitive Science Society* (pp. 1,406-1,411). Amsterdam: Cognitive Science Society. Available: http://cognitrn.psych.indiana.edu/rgoldsto/pdfs/day09.pdf [accessed February 22, 2010].

Dede, C. (2005). Why design-based research is both important and difficult. *Educational Technology, 45*(1), 5-8.

Dede, C. (2006). *Online professional development for teachers: Emerging models and methods*. Cambridge, MA: Harvard Education Press.

Dede, C. (2009a). Immersive interfaces for engagement and learning. *Science, 323*(5910), 66-69.

Dede, C. (2009b). Technologies that facilitate generating knowledge and possibly wisdom: A response to "Web 2.0 and classroom research." *Educational Researcher, 38*(4), 60-63.

Dede, C. (2009c). *Learning context: Gaming, gaming simulations, and science learning in the classroom*. Paper commissioned for the National Research Council Workshop on Gaming and Simulations, October 6-7, Washington, DC. Available: http://www7.nationalacademies.org/bose/Dede_Gaming_CommissionedPaper. pdf [accessed February 2011].

Dede, C., and Ketelhut, D.J. (2003). *Designing for motivation and usability in a museum-based multi-user virtual environment*. Paper presented at the American Educational Research Association Conference, Chicago.

Dede, C., Ketelhut, D.J., and Ruess, K. (2002). Motivation, usability, and learning outcomes in a prototype museum-based multi-user virtual environment. In *Proceedings of the Fifth International Conference on the Learning Sciences* (pp. 406-408). Mahwah, NJ: Lawrence Erlbaum.

Dede, C., Honan, J., and Peters. L. (Eds). (2005). *Scaling up success: Lessons learned from technology-based educational innovation*. New York: Jossey-Bass.

de Jong, T. (2005). The guided discovery principle in multimedia learning. In R.E. Mayer (Ed.), *The Cambridge handbook of multimedia learning* (pp. 215-228). New York: Cambridge University Press.

de Jong, T. (2006). Technological advances in inquiry learning. *Science, 312*, 532-533. Available: http://www.sciencemag.org/cgi/content/full/312/5773/532 [accessed March 3, 2010].

de Jong, T. (2009). *Learning with computer simulations: Evidence and future directions*. Presentation to the National Research Council Workshop on Gaming and Simulations, October 6-7, Washington, DC. Available: http://www7.nationalacademies. org/bose/deJong_Gaming_Presentation.pdf [accessed February 15, 2011].

DeVane, B., Durga, S., and Squire, K.D. (2009). Competition as a driver for learning. *International Journal of Learning and Media, 1*(2).

Dieterle, E. (2009). Neomillennial learning styles and River City. *Children, Youth and Environments, 19*(1), 245278.

Dieterle, E., Dede, C., Clarke, J., Dukas, G., Garduño, E., and Ketelhut, D.J. (2008). *Formative assessments integrated into a MUVE that provides real-time feedback for teachers on student learning.* Paper presented at the 2008 American Educational Research Association Conference, New York, NY.

Digital Youth Network. (2010). *Current research projects.* Available: http://iremix. org/3-research/pages/5-current-research-findings [accessed March 17, 2010].

diSessa, A.A. (1993). Toward an epistemology of physics. *Cognition and Instruction, 10*(2-3), 105-225.

diSessa, A.A., Hammer, D.M., Sherin, B., and Kolpakowski, T. (1991). Inventing graphing: Children's meta-representational expertise. *Journal of Mathematical Behavior, 10*(2), 117.

Doerr, H. (1996). Integrating the study of trigonometry, vectors, and force through modeling. *School Science and Mathematics, 96*, 407-418.

Dunleavy, M., Dede, C., and Mitchell, R. (2009). Affordances and limitations of immersive participatory augmented reality simulations for teaching and learning. *Journal of Science Education and Technology, 18*(1 February), 7-22.

Durkin, K. (2006). Game playing and adolescents' development. In P. Vorderer and J. Bryant (Eds.), *Playing video games: Motives, responses, and consequences* (pp. 415-428). Mahwah, NJ: Lawrence Erlbaum.

Duschl, R. (2004). *The HS lab experience: Reconsidering the role of evidence, explanation, and the language of science.* Paper prepared for the Committee on High School Science Laboratories: Role and Vision. Available: http://www7. nationalacademies.org/bose/July_12-13_2004_High_School_Labs_Meeting_ Agenda.html [accessed December 14, 2004].

Dye, M.W.G., Green, C.S., and Bavelier, D. (2009). Increasing speed of processing with action video games. *Current Directions in Psychological Science, 18*(6), 321-326.

Edelson, D.C., Gordin, D.N., and Pea, R.D. (1999). Addressing the challenges of inquiry-based learning through technology and curriculum design. *Journal of the Learning Sciences, 8*(3/4), 391-450.

Edelson, D.C., Salierno, C., Matese, G., Pitts, V., and Sherin, B. (2002). *Learning-for-use in earth science: Kids as climate modelers.* Paper presented at the annual meeting of the National Association for Research in Science Teaching, New Orleans, April.

Entertainment Software Association. (2010). *Industry facts.* Available: http://www. theesa.com/facts/index.asp [accessed April 19, 2010].

Evans, K.L., Yaron, D., and Leinhardt, G. (2008). Learning stoichiometry: A comparison of text and multimedia formats. *Chemistry Education Research and Practice, 9*, 208-218. Available: http://oli.web.cmu.edu/openlearning/publications/110 [accessed September 23, 2010].

Falk, J., and Drayton, B. (Eds.). (2009). *Creating and sustaining online professional learning communities.* New York: Teachers College Press.

Federation of American Scientists. (2007). *Harnessing the power of video games for learning.* Washington, DC: Author. Available: http://www.fas.org/gamesummit/ Resources/Summit%20on%20Educational%20Games.pdf [accessed January 2010].

Fletcher, J.D. (2009a). Education and training technology in the military. *Science, 323,* 72-75. Available: http://www.sciencemag.org/cgi/reprint/sci;323/5910/72. pdf?ck=nck [accessed February 23, 2010].

Fletcher, J.D. (2009b).*Training via simulations and games.* Presentation to the National Research Council Workshop on Gaming and Simulations, October 6-7, Washington, DC. Available: http://www7.nationalacademies.org/bose/Fletcher_Gaming_Presentation.pdf [accessed February 23, 2010].

Frederiksen, J.R., White, B.Y., and Gutwill, J. (1999). Dynamic mental models in learning science: The importance of constructing derivational linkages among models. *Journal of Research in Science Teaching, 36*(7), 806-836.

Frezzo, D.C., Behrens, J.T., and Mislevy, R.J. (in press). Design patterns for learning and assessment: Facilitating the introduction of a complex simulation-based learning environment into a community of instructors. *Journal of Science Education and Technology.*

Gershenfeld, A. (2009). *Bringing game-based learning to scale: The business challenges of serious games.* Paper commissioned for the National Research Council Workshop on Gaming and Simulations, October 6-7, Washington, DC. Available: http://www7.nationalacademies.org/bose/Gershenfeld_Gaming_CommissionedPaper.pdf [accessed April 12, 2010].

Giacquinta, J.B., Bauer, J.A., and Levin, J.E. (1993). *Beyond technology's promise: An examination of children's educational computing in the home.* Cambridge, UK: Cambridge University Press.

Gibson, H., and Chase, C. (2002). Longitudinal impact of an inquiry-based science program on middle school students' attitudes toward science. *Science Education, 86*(5), 693-705.

Goldman, K.H., Koepfler, J., and Yocco, V. (2009). *WolfQuest summative evaluation: Full summative report.* Edgewater, MD: Institute for Learning Innovation. Available: http://www.informalscience.org/reports/0000/0206/WQ_Full_Summative_Report.pdf [accessed April 26, 2010].

Green, C.S., and Bavelier, D. (2006). Effect of action video games on the spatial distribution of visuospatial attention. *Journal of Experimental Psychology: Human Perception and Performance, 32*(6), 1,465-1,468.

Grigg, W.S., Lauko, M.A., and Brockway, D.M. (2006). *The nation's report card: Science 2005.* Washington, DC: National Center for Education Statistics.

Hamilton, L. (2003). Assessment as a policy tool. *Review of Research in Education, 27,* 25-68.

Hattie, J., Jaeger, R., and Bond, L. (1999). Persistent methodological questions in educational testing. *Review of Research in Education, 24,* 393-446.

Hansen, E.G., Zapata-Rivera, D., and Feng, M. (2009). *Beyond accessibility: Evidence centered design for improving the efficiency of learning-centered assessments.* Paper presented at the annual meeting of the National Council on Measurement in Education, April 16, San Diego.

Hayes, E.R., and King, E.M. (2009). Not just a dollhouse: What *The Sims2* can teach us about women's IT learning. *On The Horizon, 17*(1), 60-69.

Hays, R.T. (2005). *The effectiveness of instructional games: A literature review and discussion.* (Technical Report No. 2005-004). Orlando, FL: Naval Air Warfare Center Training Systems Division.

Henderson, C., and Dancy, M.H. (2009). Impact of physics education research on the teaching of introductory quantitative physics in the United States. *Physical Review Special Topics—Physics Education Research, 5*(2). Available: http://prst-per.aps. org/pdf/PRSTPER/v5/i2/e020107 [accessed May 3, 2010].

Hickey, D., Ingram-Goble, A., and Jameson, E. (2009). Designing assessments and assessing designs in virtual educational environments. *Journal of Science Education and Technology, 18*(2), 187-208.

Hickey, D.T., Kindfield, A.C.H., Horwitz, P., and Christie, M.A.T. (2003). Integrating curriculum, instruction, assessment, and evaluation in a technology-supported genetics learning environment. *American Educational Research Journal, 40*(2), 495-538.

Hight, J. (2009). *Challenges of bringing gaming and simulations to scale for science learning.* Presentation to the National Research Council Workshop on Gaming and Simulations, October 6-7, Washington, DC. Available: http:// www7.nationalacademies.org/bose/Hight_Gaming_Presentation.pdf [accessed March 23, 2010].

Hmelo-Silver, C. E., Marathe, S., and Liu, L. (2007). Fish swim, rocks sit, and lungs breathe: Expert-novice understanding of complex systems. *Journal of the Learning Sciences, 16,* 307-331.

Hmelo-Silver, C.E., Jordan, R., Liu, L., Gray, S., Demeter, M., Rugaber, S.V., and Goel, A. (2008). Focusing on function: Thinking below the surface of complex natural systems. *Science Scope,* 27-34. Available: http://dilab.gatech.edu/publications/ Science-Scope-Paper.pdf [accessed February 2011].

Holbert, N. (2009). *Learning Newton while crashing cars.* Poster presented at the Games Learning Society Conference, Madison, WI, June, 10-12.

Horst, H. (2009). Families. In the John D. and Catherine MacArthur Foundation Series on Digital Media and Learning, M. Ito et al. (Eds.), *Hanging out, messing around, and geeking out: Kids living and learning with new media.* Cambridge, MA: MIT Press.

Horwitz, P. (2009). *Interactive curriculum and assessment: The road to scaling?* Presentation to the National Research Council Workshop on Gaming and Simulations, October 6-7, Washington, DC. Available: http://www7.nationalacademies. org/bose/Horwitz_Gaming_Presentation.pdf [accessed March 23, 2010].

Horwitz, P., Gobert, J., Buckley, B.C., and Wilensky, U. (2007). *Modeling across the curriculum: Annual report to NSF.* Concord, MA: The Concord Consortium.

Ito, M. (2009). *Sociocultural contexts of game-based learning.* Paper commissioned for the National Research Council Workshop on Gaming and Simulations, October 6-7, Washington, DC. Available: http://www7.nationalacademies.org/bose/ Gaming_Sims_Commissioned_Papers.html [accessed March 12, 2010].

Ito, M., and Bittanti, M. (2009). Gaming. In the John D. and Catherine MacArthur Foundation Series on Digital Media and Learning, M. Ito et al. (Eds.), *Hanging out, messing around, and geeking out: Kids living and learning with new media.* Cambridge, MA: MIT Press.

Ito, M., Bittanti, M., Boyd, D., Cody, R., Herr-Stephenson, B., Horst, H.A., Lange, P.G., Mahendran, D., Martinez, K.Z., Pascoe, C.J., Perkel, D., Robinson, L., Sims, C., Tripp, L., et al. (2009). *Hanging out, messing around, and geeking out: Kids living and learning with new media.* Cambridge, MA: MIT Press.

Jenkins, H., Squire, K., and Tan, P. (2004). You can't bring that game to school! Designing supercharged! In B. Laurel (Ed.), *Design research*. Cambridge, MA: MIT Press.

Kadlec, A., and Friedman, W. (2007). *Important but not for me: Parents and students in Kansas and Missouri talk about math, science, and technology education*. New York: Public Agenda. Available: http://www.publicagenda.org/reports/important-not-me [accessed January 2010].

Kafai, Y.B. (2009). *State of evidence: How can games and simulations be used to increase science learning?* Presentation to the National Research Council Workshop on Gaming and Simulations, October 6-7, Washington, DC. Available: http://www7.nationalacademies.org/bose/Kafai_Gaming_Presentation.pdf [accessed March 23, 2010].

Kafai, Y.B., and Fields, D.A. (2009). Cheating in virtual worlds: Transgressive designs for learning. *On the Horizon, 17*(1), 12-20.

Kafai, Y.B., Heeter, C., Denner, J., and Sun, J.Y (Eds.). (2008*). Beyond Barbie and Mortal Kombat: New perspectives on gender and gaming*. Cambridge, MA: MIT Press.

Kafai, Y.B., Quintero, M., and Feldon, D. (2010). Investigating the "why" in *Whypox*: Casual and systematic explorations of a virtual epidemic. *Games and Culture, 5*(1), 116-135.

Kafai, Y.B., Feldon, D., Fields, D., Giang, M., and Quintero, M. (in press). Life in the times of Whypox: A virtual epidemic as a community event. In C. Steinfeld, B. Pentland, M. Ackermann, and N. Contractor (Eds.), *Proceedings of the Third International Conference on Communities and Technology*. New York: Springer.

Kahne, J., Middaugh, E., and Evans, C. (2009). *The civic potential of video games*. Cambridge, MA: MIT Press.

Kali, Y., Linn, M.C., and Roseman, J.E. (2008). *Designing coherent science education: Implications for curriculum, instruction, and policy*. New York: Teachers College Press.

Keller, C.J., Finkelstein, N.D., Perkins, K.K., and Pollock, S.J. (2006). *Assessing the effectiveness of a computer simulation in introductory undergraduate environments*. Paper presented at the 2006 Physics Education Research Conference, July 26-27, Syracuse, NY.

Ketelhut, D.J. (2007). The impact of student self-efficacy on scientific inquiry skills: An Exploratory investigation in River City, a multi-user virtual environment. *Journal of Science Education and Technology, 16*(1), 99-111.

Ketelhut, D.J. (2009). *Rethinking science learning, a needs assessment*. Paper commissioned for the National Research Council Workshop on Gaming and Simulations, October 6-7, Washington, DC. Available: http://www7.nationalacademies.org/bose/Ketelut_Gaming_CommissionedPaper.pdf [accessed October, 2010].

Ketelhut, D.J., Dede, C., Clarke J., and Nelson, B. (2006). *A multi-user virtual environment for building higher order inquiry skills in science*. Paper presented at the 2006 AERA Annual Meeting, San Francisco, CA, April. Available: http://muve.gse.harvard.edu/rivercityproject/documents/rivercitysympinq1.pdf [accessed March 2009].

Ketelhut, D.J., Dede, C., Clarke, J., Nelson, B., and Bowman, C. (2007). Studying situated learning in a multiuser virtual environment. In E. Baker, J. Dickieson, W. Wulfeck, and H.F. O'Neil (Eds.), *Assessment of problem solving using simulations.* New York: Lawrence Erlbaum.

Ketelhut, D.J., Dede, C., Clarke, J., Nelson, B., and Bowman, C. (in press). Studying situated learning in a multi-user virtual environment. In E. Baker, J. Dickieson, W. Wulfeck, and H. O'Neil (Eds.), *Assessment of problem solving using simulations.* Mahwah, NJ: Lawrence Erlbaum.

Kirkpatrick, D.L. (1994). *Evaluating training programs: The four levels.* San Francisco: Berrett-Koehler.

Klopfer, E. (2008). *Augmented reality: Research and design of mobile educational games.* Cambridge, MA: MIT Press.

Klopfer, E., Yoon, S., and Rivas, L. (2004). Comparative analysis of palm and wearable computers for participatory simulations. *Journal of Computer Assisted Learning, 20,* 347-359.

Klopfer, E., Yoon, S., and Um, T. (2005). Teaching complex dynamic systems to young students with StarLogo. *Journal of Computers in Mathematics and Science Teaching, 24*(2), 157-178. Available: http://dl.aace.org/16982.

Klopfer, E., Scheintaub, H., Huang, W., Wendal, D., and Roque, R. (2009). The simulation cycle: Combining games, simulations, engineering and science using StarLogo TNG. *E-Learning, 6*(1), 71-96.

Kopriva, R., Gabel, D., and Bauman, J. (2009). *Building comparable computer-based science items for English learners: Results and insights from the ONPAR project.* Paper presented at the National Conference on Student Assessment (NCSA), Los Angeles, CA.

Kraiger, K., Ford, J., and Salas, E. (1993). Application of cognitive, skill-based, and affective theories of learning outcomes to new methods of training evaluation. *Journal of Applied Psychology, 78*(2), 311-328.

Krajcik, J., Marx, R., Blumenfeld, P., Soloway, E., and Fishman, B. (2000, April). *Inquiry-based science supported by technology: Achievement and motivation among urban middle school students.* Paper presented at the annual meeting of the American Educational Research Association, New Orleans.

Kutner, L., and Olson, C.K. (2008). *Grand theft childhood: The surprising truth about violent video games and what parents can do.* New York: Simon & Schuster.

Lareau, A. (2003). *Unequal childhoods; Class, race, and family life.* Berkeley: University of California Press.

Lesgold, A. (2001). The nature and methods of learning by doing. *American Psychologist, 56*(11), 964-973.

Lesgold, A.M., Lajoie, S.P., Bunzo, M., and Eggan, G. (1992). SHERLOCK: A coached practice environment for an electronics troubleshooting job. In J. Larkin and R. Chabay (Eds.), *Computer-assisted instruction and intelligent tutoring systems: Shared issues and complementary approaches* (pp. 201-238). Hillsdale, NJ: Lawrence Erlbaum.

Lewis, E.L., Stern, J., and Linn, M.C. (1993). The effect of computer simulations on introductory thermodynamics understanding. *Educational Technology, 33*(1), 45-58.

Li, R., Polat, U., Makous, W., and Bavelier, D. (2009). Enhancing the contrast sensitivity function through action video game training. *Nature Neuroscience, 2296.* Available: http://www.bcs.rochester.edu/people/Daphne/Li_NN.pdf [accessed February 22, 2010].

Lindgren, R., and Schwartz, D.L. (2009). Spatial learning and computer simulations in science. *International Journal of Science Education, 31*(3), 419-438.

Linn, M.C. and Eylon, B.-S. (in press). *Science learning and instruction: Taking advantage of technology to promote knowledge integration.* New York: Routledge.

Linn, M.C., and Hsi, S. (2000). *Computers, teachers, peers: Science learning partners.* Mahwah, NJ: Lawrence Erlbaum.

Linn, M.C., Chang, H-Y., Chiu, J., Zhang, H., and McElhaney, K. (2010). Can desirable difficulties overcome deception clarity in scientific visualizations? In A.S. Benjamin (Ed.) *Successful remembering and successful forgetting: A Festschrift in honor of Robert A. Bjork.* New York: Routledge.

Linn, M.D., Lewis, C., Tsuchida, I., and Songer, N.B. (2000). Beyond fourth-grade science: Why do U.S. and Japanese students diverge? *Educational Researcher, 29*(3), 4-14.

Linn, R. (1998). Validating inferences from National Assessment of Educational Progress achievement-level reporting. *Applied Measurement in Education, 11*(1), 23-47.

Ma, J., and Nickerson, J.V. (2006). Hands-on, simulated, and remote laboratories: A comparative literature review. *ACM Computing Surveys, 38*(3), 1-24.

Ma, X., and Ma, L. (2004). Modeling stability of growth between mathematics and science achievement during middle and high school. *Evaluation Review, 28*(2), 104-122.

Ma, X., and Wilkins, J.L. (2002). The development of science achievement in middle and high schools: Individual differences and school effects. *Evaluation Review, 26*(4), 395-417.

Mandinach, E., and Cline, H. (1993). Systems, science and schools. *System Dynamics Review, 9*(2), 195-206.

Martin, J., and VanLehn, K. (1995). Student assessment using Bayesian nets. *International Journal of Human-Computer Studies, 42,* 575-591.

Massachusetts Institute of Technology, Center for Future Civic Media. (2010). *TimeLab 2100.* Available: http://civic.mit.edu/projects/c4fcm/timelab-2100 [accessed February 4, 2010].

Mayer, R.C. (2004). Should there be a three-strikes rule against pure discovery learning? The case for guided methods of instruction. *American Psychologist, 59*(1), 14-19.

Mayer, R.E., Mautone, P., and Prothero, W. (2002). Pictorial aids for learning by doing in a multimedia geology simulation game. *Journal of Educational Psychology, 94,* 171-185.

Mayo, M.J. (2009a). Video games: A route to large-scale STEM education? *Science, 323.* Available: http://www.sciencemag.org/cgi/content/full/323/5910/79 [accessed April 5, 2010].

Mayo, M.J. (2009b). *Bringing game-based learning to scale: The business challenges of serious gaming.* Paper presented at the National Research Council Workshop on Gaming and Simulations, October 6-7, Washington, DC. Available: http://www7. nationalacademies.org/bose/Mayo_Gaming_CommissionedPaper.pdf [accessed April 5, 2010].

McQuiggan, S.W., Robison, J.L., and Lester, J.C. (2008). *Affective transitions in narrative-centered learning environments.* Paper presented at the Proceedings of the Ninth International Conference on Intelligent Tutoring Systems, Montreal, Canada.

Meir, E., Perry, J., Stal, D., Maruca, S., and Klopfer, E. (2005). How effective are simulated molecular1 level experiments for teaching diffusion and osmosis? *Cell Biology Education, 4,* 235-248.

Messick, S. (1994). The interplay of evidence and consequences in the validation of performance assessments. *Educational Researcher, 32,* 13-23.

Metcalf, S.J., Clarke, J. and Dede, C. (2009). *Virtual worlds for education: River city and EcoMUVE.* Paper presented at the Media in Transition International Conference, MIT, April 24-26, Cambridge, MA.

Meyer, A., and Rose, D.H. (2005). The future is in the margins: The role of technology and disability in educational reform. In D.H. Rose, A. Meyer, and C. Hitchcock (Eds.), *The universally designed classroom: Accessible curriculum and digital technologies* (pp. 13-35). Cambridge, MA: Harvard Education Press.

Mitchell, T.M. (1997). *Machine Learning.* New York: McGraw-Hill.

Miller, J.D. (1998). The measurement of civic scientific literacy. *Public Understanding of Science, 7*(3), 203-223.

Miller, J.D. (2001). The acquisition and retention of scientific information by American adults. In J.H. Falk (Ed.), *Free-choice science education: How we learn science outside of school* (pp. 93-114). New York: Teachers College Press.

Miller, J.D. (2002). Civic scientific literacy: A necessity for the 21st century. *Public Interest Report: Journal of the Federation of American Scientists, 55*(1), 3-6.

Miller, J.D., Pardo, R., and Niwa, F. (1997). *Public perceptions of science and technology: A comparative study of the European Union, the United States, Japan, and Canada.* Madrid: BBV Foundation Press.

Mislevy, R.J., and Gitomer, D.H. (1996). The role of probability-based inference in an intelligent tutoring system. *User-Modeling and User-Adapted Interaction, 5,* 253-282.

Mislevy, R.J., Chudowsky, N., Draney, K., Fried, R., Gaffney, T., Haertel, G., Hafter, A., Hamel, L., Kennedy, C., Long, K., Morrison, A.L., Murphy, R., Pena, P., Quellmalz, E., Rosenquist, A., Songer, N., Schank, P., Wenk, A., and Wilson, M. (2003). *Design patterns for assessing science inquiry* (PADI Technical Report 1). Menlo Park, CA: SRI International, Center for Technology in Learning.

Moreno, R., and Mayer, R.E. (2000). Engaging students in active learning: The case for personalized multimedia messages. *Journal of Educational Psychology, 92,* 724-733.

Moreno, R., and Mayer, R.E. (2004). Personalized messages that promote science learning in virtual environments. *Journal of Educational Psychology, 96,* 165-173.

Moreno, R., and Mayer, R.E. (2005). Role of guidance, reflection, and interactivity in an agent-based multimedia game. *Journal of Educational Psychology, 97,* 117-128.

Moreno, R., and Mayer, R.E. (2007). Interactive multimodal learning environments. *Educational Psychology Review, 19*(3), 309-326.

Motion Picture Association of America. (2010). *Research and statistics.* Available: http://www.mpaa.org/researchStatistics.asp [accessed April 19, 2010].

National Academy of Sciences, National Academy of Engineering, and Institute of Medicine. (2007). *Rising above the gathering storm: Energizing and employing America for a brighter economic future.* Committee on Prospering in the Global Economy of the 21st Century: An Agenda for American Science and Technology. Washington, DC: The National Academies Press.

National Center for Education Statistics. (2007). *Special Analysis 2007: High school coursetaking.* Table SA-4C. Available: http://nces.ed.gov/programs/coe/2007/analysis/sa_table.asp?tableID=825 [accessed February 24, 2010].

National Research Council. (2000). *How people learn: Brain, mind, experience, and school: Expanded edition.* Committee on Developments in the Science of Learning with additional material from the Committee on Learning Research and Educational Practice. Washington, DC: National Academy Press.

National Research Council. (2001). *Knowing what students know: The science and design of educational assessment.* Committee on the Foundations of Assessment, J.W. Pellegrino, N. Chudowsky, and R.G. Glaser (Eds.). Washington, DC: National Academy Press.

National Research Council. (2002). *Performance assessments for adult education: Exploring the measurement issues, Report of a workshop.* Committee for the Workshop on Alternatives for Assessing Adult Education and Literacy Programs, R. J. Mislevy and K.T. Knowles (Eds.). Board on Testing and Assessment, Center for Education, Division of Behavioral and Social Sciences and Education. Washington, DC: The National Academies Press.

National Research Council. (2004). *Engaging schools: Fostering high school students' motivation to learn.* Committee on Increasing High School Students' Engagement and Motivation to Learn. Washington, DC: The National Academies Press.

National Research Council. (2005a). *How students learn: History, mathematics, and science in the classroom.* Committee on How People Learn, A Targeted Report for Teachers, Center for Studies on Behavior and Development. Washington, DC: The National Academies Press.

National Research Council (2005b). *America's lab report: Investigations in high school science.* Committee on High School Science Laboratories: Role and Vision, S.R. Singer, M.L. Hilton, and H.A. Schweingruber (Eds.). Washington, DC: The National Academies Press.

National Research Council. (2006). *Systems for state science assessment.* Committee on Test Design for K-12 Science Achievement, M.R. Wilson and M.W. Bertenthal (Eds.). Washington, DC: The National Academies Press.

National Research Council. (2007). *Taking science to school: Teaching and learning science in grades K-8.* Committee on Science Learning, Kindergarten Through Eighth Grade, R.A. Duschl, H.A. Schweingruber, and A.W. Shouse (Eds.). Washington, DC: The National Academies Press.

National Research Council. (2009). *Learning science in informal environments: People, places, and pursuits.* Committee on Learning Science in Informal Environments, P. Bell, B. Lewenstein, A.W. Shouse, and M.A. Feder (Eds.). Washington, DC: The National Academies Press.

National Research Council. (2010). *The rise of games and high-performance computing for modeling and simulation.* Committee on Modeling, Simulation, and Games. Division on Engineering and Physical Sciences. Washington, DC: The National Academies Press.

Nelson, B. (2007). Exploring the use of individualized, reflective guidance in an educational multi-user virtual environment. *Journal of Science Education and Technology, 16*(1), 83-97.

Neulight, N., Kafai, Y.B., Kao, L., Foley, B., and Galas, C. (2007). Children's participation in a virtual epidemic in the science classroom: Making connections to natural infectious diseases. *Journal of Science Education and Technology, 16*(1), 47-58.

Nichols, S., and Berliner, D. (2008a). Why has high-stakes testing so easily slipped into contemporary American life? *Phi Delta Kappan, 89*(9), 672-676.

Nichols, S., and Berliner, D. (2008b). Testing the joy out of learning. *Educational Leadership, 65*(6), 14-18.

Nulty, A., and Shaffer, D.W. (2008). *Digital zoo: The effects of mentoring on young engineers.* Paper presented at the International Conference of the Learning Sciences (ICLS), Utrecht, Netherlands.

O'Neil, H.F., Wainess, R., and Baker, E.L. (2005). Classification of learning outcomes: Evidence from the computer games literature. *Curriculum Journal, 16,* 455-474.

Organisation for Economic Co-operation and Development. (2007). *Programme for International Student Assessment (PISA) 2006: Science competencies for tomorrow's world* (vol. I). Paris: Author. Available: http://www.oecd.org/document/2/0,3343,en_32252351_32236191_39718850_1_1_1_1,00.html [accessed July 28, 2010].

Osterweil, S. (2009). *Bringing game-based learning to scale: A response.* Paper commissioned for the National Research Council Workshop on Gaming and Simulations, October 6-7, Washington, DC. Available: http://www7.nationalacademies.org/bose/Osterweil_Gaming_CommissionedPaper.pdf [accessed April 12, 2010].

Parnafes, O. (2007). What does "fast" mean? Understanding the physical world through computational representations. *Journal of the Learning Sciences, 16*(3), 415-450.

Partnership for Reform in Science and Mathematics. (2005). *Georgia students rank parents as primary influencers in student success.* Available: http://www.gaprism.org/media/news/112905.pdf [accessed January 2010].

Pew Research Center and American Association for the Advancement of Science. (2009). *Public praises science, scientists fault public, media; a survey.* Available: http://people-press.org/reports/pdf/528.pdf [accessed September 27, 2009].

Pitaru, A. (2008). E is for everyone: The case for inclusive game design. In K. Salen (Ed.), *The ecology of games: Connecting youth, games, and learning* (pp. 67-88). Cambridge, MA: MIT Press.

Plass, J.L., Homer, B.D., Milne, C., Jordan, T., Kim, M., and Barrientos, J. (2007). *Representational mode and cognitive load: Optimizing the instructional design of science simulations.* Featured research paper presented at the annual convention of the Association for Educational Communication and Technology, October, Anaheim, CA.

Plass, J.L., Homer, B.D., and Hayward, E.O. (2009). Design factors for educationally effective animations and simulations. *Journal of Computing in Higher Education, 21,* 31-61.

Plass, J.L., Goldman, R., Flanagan, M., and Perlin, K. (2009). RAPUNSEL: Improving self-efficacy and self-esteem with an educational computer game. In S.C. Kong, H. Ogata, H.C. Amseth, C.K.K. Chan, T. Hirashama, F. Klett, J.H.M. Lee, C.C. Liu, C.K. Looi, M. Milrad, A. Mitrovic, K. Nakabayashi, S.L. Wong, and S.J.H. Yang (Eds.), *Proceedings of the 17th International Conference on Computers in Education (CDROM).* Hong Kong: Asia-Pacific Society for Computers in Education.

Project Tomorrow and PASCO Scientific. (2008). *Inspiring the next generation of innovators: Students, parents, and teachers speak up about science education.* Irvine, CA: Author. Available: http://www.tomorrow.org/SpeakUp/pdfs/Inspiring_the_next_generation_of_innovators.pdf [accessed February 3, 2010].

Quellmalz, E.S., and Haertel, G. (2004). *Technology supports for state science assessment systems.* Paper commissioned by the National Research Council Committee on Test Design for K-12 Science Achievement. Washington, DC: The National Academies Press.

Quellmalz, E.S., and Haertel, G.D. (2008). Assessing new literacies in science and mathematics. In D.J. Leu, Jr., J. Coiro, M. Knowbel, and C. Lankshear (Eds.), *Handbook of research on new literacies.* Mahwah, NJ: Lawrence Erlbaum.

Quellmalz, E.S., and Pellegrino, J.W. (2009). Technology and testing. *Science, 323,* 75-79.

Quellmalz, E.S., DeBarger, A., Haertel, G., and Kreikemeier, P. (2005). *Validities of science inquiry assessments: Final report.* Menlo Park, CA: SRI International.

Quellmalz, E.S., DeBarger, A.H., Haertel, G., Schank, P., Buckley, B., Gobert, J., Horwitz, P., and Ayala, C. (2008). *Exploring the role of technology-based simulations in science assessment: The Calipers Project.* Presented at American Educational Research Association (AERA) 2007, Chicago, IL. In *Science assessment: Research and practical approaches.* Arlington, VA: NSTA.

Quellmalz, E.S., Timms, M.J., and Schneider, S.A. (2009). *Assessment of student learning in science simulations and games.* Paper commissioned for the National Research Council Workshop on Gaming and Simulations, October 6-7, Washington, DC. Available: http://www7.nationalacademies.org/bose/Schneider_Gaming_CommissionedPaper.pdf [accessed March 23, 2010].

Quellmalz, E.S., Timms, M.J., and Buckley, B.C. (in press). The promise of simulation-based science assessment: The calipers project. *International Journal of Learning Technologies.*

Raghavan, K., and Glaser, R. (1995). Model-based analysis and reasoning in science: The MARS curriculum. *Science Education, 79*(1), 37-61.

Resnick, M., Rusk, N., and Cooke, S. (1998). The Computer Clubhouse: Technological fluency in the inner city. In D. Schon, B. Sanyal, and W. Mitchell (Eds.), *High technology and low-income communities.* Cambridge, MA: MIT Press.

Resnick, M., Maloney, J., Monroy-Hernandez, A., Rusk, N., Eastmond, E., Brennan, K., Millner, A., Rosenbaum, E., Silver, J., Silverman, B., and Kafai, Y. (2009). Scratch: Programming for all. *Communications of the ACM, 52*(11), 60-67.

Richards, J., Barowy, W., and Levin, D. (1992). Computer simulation in the science classroom. *Journal of Science Education and Technology, 1*(1), 67-79.

Rideout, V.G., Foehr, U.G., and Roberts, D.F. (2010). *Generation M2: Media in the lives of 8- to 18-year-olds.* Menlo Park, CA: Kaiser Family Foundation. Available: http://www.kff.org/entmedia/upload/8010.pdf [accessed January 2010].

Rieber, L.P., Tzeng, S., and Tribble, K. (2004). Discovery learning, representation, and explanation within a computer-based simulation. *Computers and Education, 27*(1), 45-58.

Roberts, D.F., and Foehr, U.G. (2008). Trends in media use. *The Future of Children, 18*(1), 11-37.

Robison, J., McQuiggan, S., and Lester, J. (2009). *Evaluating the consequences of affective feedback in intelligent tutoring systems.* Paper presented at the Proceedings of the International Conference on Affective Computing and Intelligent Interaction, Amsterdam, Netherlands.

Rogers, C., and Portsmore, M. (2004). Engineering in the elementary school. *Journal of STEM Education, 5*(3/4), 17-28.

Roschelle, J. (1991). *Students' construction of qualitative physics knowledge: Learning about velocity and acceleration in a computer microworld.* Unpublished doctoral dissertation, University of California, Berkeley.

Roschelle, J. (2003). Unlocking the learning value of wireless mobile devices. *Journal of Computer Assisted Learning, 19*(3), 260-272.

Roschelle, J., Patton, C., and Tatar, D. (2007). Designing networked handheld devices to enhance school learning. In M. Zelkowitz (Ed.), *Advances in computers* (vol. 70, pp. 1-60). Burlington, MA: Academic Press.

Rosenbaum, E., Klopfer, E., and Perry, J. (2006). On location learning: Authentic applied science with networked augmented realities. *Journal of Science Education and Technology, 16*(1), 31-45.

Rothberg, M.A., Sandberg, S., and Awerbuch, T.E. (1994). Educational software for simulating risk of HIV infection. *Journal of Science Education and Technology, 3*(1), 65-70.

Sandoval, W.A. (2003). Conceptual and epistemic aspects of students' scientific explanations. *Journal of the Learning Sciences, 12*(1), 5-51.

Sandoval, W.A., and Reiser, B.J. (2004).Explanation-driven inquiry: Integrating conceptual and epistemic scaffolds for scientific inquiry. *Science Education, 88*, 345-372.

Scalise, K., Timms, M., Clark, L., and Moorjani, A. (2009). *Student learning in science simulations: What makes a difference?* Paper presented at the Session on "Conversation, Argumentation, and Engagement and Science Learning," American Educational Research Association Annual Conference, April 14, San Diego, CA.

Schaller, D.T., Goldman, K.H., Spikelmeier, G., Allison-Bunnell, S., and Koepfer, J. (2009). Learning in the wild: What WolfQuest taught developers and game players. In J. Trant and D. Bearman (Eds.), *Museums and the web 2009: Proceedings.* Toronto: Archives and Museum Informatics. Available: http://www.archimuse.com/mw2009/papers/schaller/schaller.html [accessed February 24, 2010].

Schwartz, D.L., Bransford, J.D., and Sears, D. (2005). Efficiency and innovation in transfer. In J.P. Mestre (Ed.), *Transfer of learning from a multidisciplinary perspective* (pp. 1-51). Greenwich, CT: Information Age.

Schwartz, D.L., Chase, C., Chin, C., Oppezzo, M., Kwong, H., Okita, S., Biswas, G., Roscoe, R.D., Jeong, H., and Wagster, J.D. (2007). Interactive metacognition: Monitoring and regulating a teachable agent. In D.J. Hacker, J. Dunlosky, and A.C. Graesser (Eds.), *Handbook of Metacognition and Education.* New York: Routledge.

Schwarz, C., and White, B. (2005). Meta-modeling knowledge: Developing students' understanding of scientific modeling. *Cognition and Instruction, 23*(2), 165-205.

Schwarz, C., Meyer, J., and Sharma, A. (2007). Technology, pedagogy, and epistemology: Opportunities and challenges of using computer modeling and simulation tools in elementary science methods. *Journal of Science Teacher Education, 18*(2), 243-269.

Seiter, E. (2005). *The Internet playground: Children's access, entertainment, and mis-education.* New York: Peter Lang.

Seiter, E. (2007). Practicing at home: Computers, pianos, and cultural capital. In T. McPherson (Ed.), *Digital youth, innovation, and the unexpected.* The John D. and Catherine T. MacArthur Foundation Series on Digital Media and Learning. Cambridge, MA: MIT Press.

Sengupta, P., and Wilensky, U. (2006) *NIELS: An agent-based modeling environment for learning electromagnetism.* Paper presented at the annual meeting of the American Educational Research Association, San Francisco.

Sengupta, P., and Wilensky, U. (2008a). *Designing across ages: On the low-threshold-high-ceiling nature of NetLogo based learning environments.* Paper presented at the annual meeting of the American Educational Research Association (AERA 2008), New York.

Sengupta, P., and Wilensky, U. (2008b). On the learnability of electricity as a complex system. In M. Jacobson (Chair) and R. Noss (Discussant), Complex systems and learning: Empirical research, issues and "seeing" scientific knowledge with new eyes. In *Proceedings of the International Conference for the Learning Sciences.*

Sengupta, P., and Wilensky, U. (2009). Learning electricity with NIELS: Thinking with electrons and thinking in levels. *International Journal of Computers for Mathematical Learning, 14*(1), 21-50.

Shaffer, D. (2006). Epistemic frames for epistemic games. *Computers and Education, 46*(3), 223-234.

Shaul, M.S., and Ganson, H.C. (2005). The No Child Left Behind Act of 2001: The federal government's role in strengthening accountability for student performance. *Review of Research in Education, 29,* 151-165.

Shepard, L.A. (1997). Children not ready to learn? The invalidity of school readiness testing. *Psychology in the Schools, 34*(2), 85-97.

Shepard, L.A. (2002). The hazards of high-stakes testing. *Issues in Science and Technology, 19*(2), 53.

Shute, V.J., Masduki,I., Donmez, O., Dennen, V.P., Kim, Y.-J., Jeong, A.C., and Wang, C.-Y. (2009). Modeling, assessing, and supporting key competencies within game environments. In D. Ifenthaler, P. Pirnay-Dummer, and N.M. Seel (Eds.), *Computer-based diagnostics and systematic analysis of knowledge* (pp. 281-310). New York: Springer-Verlag.

Sloane, F., and Kelly, A. (2003). Issues in high-stakes testing programs. *Theory Into Practice, 42*(1), 12-17.

Smith, M., and Fey, P. (2000). Validity and accountability in high-stakes testing. *Journal of Teacher Education, 51*(5), 334-344.

Son, J.Y., and Goldstone, R.L. (2009). Fostering general transfer with specific simulations. *Pragmatics and Cognition, 17*, 1-42.

Songer, N.B. (2009). *Design principles for deep thinking about science with simulations.* Presentation to the National Research Council Workshop on Gaming and Simulations, October 6-7, Washington, DC. Available: http://www7.nationalacademies. org/bose/Songer_Gaming_Presentation.pdf [accessed March 23, 2010].

Songer, N.B., Kelcey, B., and Gotwals, A.W. (2009). *How and when does complex reasoning occur: Empirically driven development of a learning progression focused on complex reasoning about biodiversity.* Paper presented at the annual meeting of the American Education Research Association, San Diego, April. Available: http://www.biokids.umich.edu/papers/songerkelceygotwalsAERA4.09.pdf [accessed March 10, 2010].

Squire, K. (2008a). Open-ended video games: A model for developing learning in the interactive age. In K. Salen (Ed.), *The John D. and Catherine T. MacArthur Foundation series on digital media and learning* (pp. 167-198). Cambridge, MA: MIT Press.

Squire, K. (2008b). Designing centers of expertise for academic learning through video games. *Theory Into Practice, 47*(3), 240-251.

Squire, K., and Durga, S. (in press). Productive gaming: The case for historiographic game play. In R. Ferdig (Ed.), *The handbook of educational gaming.* Hershey, PA: Information Science Reference.

Squire, K., and Klopfer, E. (2007). Augmented reality simulations on handheld computers. *Journal of the Learning Sciences, 16*(3), 371-413.

Squire, K., and Patterson, N. (2009). *Games and simulations in informal science education.* Paper commissioned for the National Research Council Workshop on Gaming and Simulations, October 6-7, Washington, DC. Available: http://www7. nationalacademies.org/bose/Gaming_Sims_Commissioned_Papers.html [accessed March 12, 2010].

Squire, K.D. (2010). From information to experience: Place-based augmented reality games as a model for learning in a globally networked society. *Teachers College Record, 112*(10), 4-5.

Squire, K.D., and Jan, M. (2007). Mad City Mystery: Developing scientific argumentation skills with a place-based augmented reality game on handheld computers. *Journal of Science Education and Technology, 16*(1) 5-29.

Squire, K.D., DeVane, B., and Durga, S. (in press). Designing centers of expertise for academic learning through video games. *Theory Into Practice.*

Steinkuehler, C. (2006). Virtual worlds, learning, and the new pop cosmopolitanism. *Teachers College Record,* 12843.

Steinkuehler, C. (2008). Massively multiplayer online games as an educational technology: An outline for research. *Educational Technology, 48*(1), 10-21.

Steinkuehler, C., and King, B. (2009). Digital literacies for the disengaged: Creating after school contexts to support boys' game-based literacy skills. *On the Horizon, 17*(1), 47-59.

Steinkuehler, C.A. (2005). The new third place: Massively multiplayer online gaming in American youth culture. *Tidskrift Journal of Research in Teacher Education, 3*, 17-32.

Steinkuehler, D., and Duncan, S. (2008). Scientific habits of mind in virtual worlds. *Journal of Science Education and Technology, 17*(6), 530-543.

Stevens, R., Beal, C., and Sprang M., (2009). *Developing versatile automated assessments of scientific problem solving.* Presentation to the National Research Council Workshop on Gaming and Simulations, October 6-7, Washington, DC. Available: http://www7.nationalacademies.org/bose/Songer_Gaming_Presentation.pdf [accessed March 23, 2010].

Stevens, R., Satwicz, T., and McCarthy, L. (2008). In-game, in-room, in-world: Reconnecting video game play to the rest of kids' lives. In K. Salen (Ed.), *The ecology of games: Connecting youth, games, and learning* (pp. 41-66). Cambridge, MA: MIT Press.

Thai, A.M., Lowenstein, D., Ching, D., and Rejeski, D. (2009). *Game changer: Investing in digital play to advance children's learning and health.* New York: The Joan Ganz Cooney Center at Sesame Workshop. Available: http://www.joanganzcooneycenter.org/pdf/Game_Changer_FINAL.pdf [accessed January 2010].

Thomas, D., and Brown, J. (2007). The play of imagination: Extending the literary mind. *Games and Culture, 2*(2), 149.

Timms, M. (2007). Using item response theory (IRT) in an intelligent tutoring system. Proceedings of the 2007 Artificial Intelligence in Education Conference, Marina Del Ray, CA. *Frontiers in Artificial Intelligence and* Applications (vol. 158, pp. 213-221). Amsterdam, Netherlands: IOS Press.

Tuzan, H. (2004). *Motivating learners in educational computer games.* Bloomington: Indiana University.

U.S. Department of Education. (2010). *Transforming American education: Learning powered by technology.* Draft National Education Technology Plan. Washington, DC: Author. Available: http://www.ed.gov/technology/netp-2010 [accessed July 28, 2010].

U.S. President. (2009). *President Obama addresses NAS annual meeting.* Washington, DC Available: http://www.nationalacademies.org/morenews/20090428.html [Accessed July 28, 2010].

Venkatesh, V., and Bala, H. (2008). Technology acceptance model 3 and a research agenda on interventions. *Decision Sciences, 39*(2008), 273-315.

Vogel, J.J., Vogel, D.S., Cannon-Bowers, J., Bowers, C.A., Muse, K., and Wright, M. (2006). Computer gaming and interactive simulations for learning: A meta-analysis. *Journal of Educational Computing Research, 34*(3), 229-243.

White, B.Y. (1993). ThinkerTools: Causal models, conceptual change, and science education. *Cognition and Instruction, 10*(1), 1-100.

White, B., and Frederiksen, J. (1998). Inquiry, modeling, and metacognition: Making science accessible to all students. *Cognition and Instruction, 16*(1), 3-118.

Wilensky, U. (1999). *NetLogo.* Center for Connected Learning and Computer-Based Modeling, Northwestern University. Available: http://ccl.northwestern.edu/ netlogo [accessed January, 2010].

Wilensky, U. (2003). Statistical mechanics for secondary school: The GasLab Modeling Toolkit. *International Journal of Computers for Mathematical Learning, 8*(1), 1-41.

Wilensky, U., and Reisman, K. (1998). Learning biology through constructing and testing computational theories—An embodied modeling approach. In Y. Bar-Yam (Ed.), P*roceedings of the Second International Conference on Complex Systems.* Nashua, NH: New England Complex Systems Institute.

Williamson, D.M., Bejar, I.I., and Mislevy, R.J. (2006). *Automated scoring of complex tasks in computer-based testing.* Mahwah, NJ: Lawrence Erlbaum.

Wilson, K.A., Bedwell, W.L., Lazzara, E.H., Salas, E., Burke, C.S., Estock, J.L., Orvis, K.L., and Conkey, C. (2009). Relationships between game attributes and learning outcomes: Review and research proposals. *Simulation Gaming, 40,* 217-266.

Woodrow Wilson Center for International Scholars. (2003). *Foresight and Governance Project explores "serious games."* Available: http://www.wilsoncenter.org/index. cfm?fuseaction=news.item&news_id=20313 [accessed November 2010].

Wulfeck, W.H., Wetzel-Smith, S.K., and Baker, E. (2007). Use of visualization techniques to improve high-stakes problem solving. In E. Baker, H.F. O'Neil, W. Wulfeck, and J. Dickiesen (2007). *Assessment of problem solving using simulations.* New York: Taylor and Francis.

Yaron, D., Karabinos, M., Lange, D., Greeno, J.G., and Leinhardt, G. (2010). The ChemCollective-Virtual Labs for Introductory Chemistry Courses. *Science, 328,* 584-585. Available: http://www.sciencemag.org/cgi/reprint/328/5978/584.pdf [accessed September 22, 2010].

Zelman, S.T. (2009). *Moving from an analog to digital culture in science education.* Presentation to the National Research Council Workshop on Gaming and Simulations, October 6-7, Washington, DC. Available: http://www7.nationalacademies. org/bose/Zelman_Gaming_Presentation.pdf [accessed March 23, 2010].

A

Commissioned Papers

All papers are available at http://www7.nationalacademies.org/bose/Gaming_Sims_Commissioned_Papers.html.

PAPERS PRESENTED ON WORKSHOP DAY 1

Rethinking Science Learning Through Digital Games and Simulations: Genres, Examples, and Evidence
    Douglas Clark, Brian Nelson, Pratim Sengupta, and Cynthia D'Angelo

Response Paper: Rethinking Science Learning: A Needs Assessment
    Diane J. Ketelhut

Learning Context: Gaming, Simulations, and Science Learning in the Classroom
    Christopher Dede

Response Paper: Gaming, Simulations, and Science Learning in the Classroom
    Katherine M. Culp

PAPERS PRESENTED ON WORKSHOP DAY 2

Games and Simulations in Informal Science Education
    Nathan Patterson and Kurt Squire

Response Paper: Sociocultural Contexts of Game-Based Learning
    Mizuko Ito

B

Workshop Agenda

LEARNING SCIENCE: GAMING, SIMULATIONS, AND EDUCATION OCTOBER 6-7, 2009

October 6, 2009

8:30 a.m.   **Welcome, Introduction of the Committee, and Overview of Workshop**
Margaret Honey, President and CEO, New York Hall of Science

9:30 a.m.   **Connections to Past and Future Board on Science Education Studies**
Heidi Schweingruber, Deputy Director, BOSE
Martin Storksdieck, Director, BOSE

9:50 a.m.   **State of the Evidence: What Kinds of Games and Simulations Support Science Learning, and Why?**
Author: Douglas Clark, Vanderbilt University
Respondent Author: Diane Ketelhut, Temple University
Committee discussion will follow.

10:50 a.m. *Break*

11:05 a.m. State of the Evidence: How Can Games and Simulations Be Used to Increase Science Learning?
        Panel:
        Yasmin Kafai, University of Pennsylvania
        Ton de Jong-Evidence of Learning, University of Twente
        Jan Plass, New York University
        Committee discussion will follow.

12:15 p.m. Participant Working Lunch
        Margaret Honey, New York Hall of Science

Guiding Questions for Participants
(2 questions will be assigned to each group):
If the participant packet code is green:
   1. What are the different genres of games and simulations for science education?
   2. How are these genres relevant to support science learning?
If the participant packet code is orange:
   3. What formal science education opportunities with games and simulations might be realized?
   4. What informal science education opportunities with games and simulations might be realized?
If the participant packet code is blue:
   5. How could games and simulations be used to support all students, regardless of individual differences (such as gender, low income), to succeed in science?
   6. What new games and simulations in science education should be built? Why?

1:15 p.m. Report Out from Participants
        Committee discussion will follow.

2:00 p.m. State of the Evidence: What Evidence Is Available from the Cognitive Sciences About Science Learning Through Games and Simulations?
        Panel:
        Daphne Bavelier, University of Rochester
        Ellen Wartella, University of California, Riverside
        Robert Goldstone, Indiana University
        Dexter Fletcher, Institute of Defense Analyses
        Committee discussion will follow.

3:00 p.m. *Break*

3:15 p.m. **Learning Context: Gaming, Simulations, and Science Learning in Formal Environments**
  Author: Chris Dede, Harvard Graduate School of Education
  Respondent Author: Katherine Culp, Education
    Development Center
  Committee discussion will follow.

4:15 p.m. **Panel Discussion of Learning Context: Gaming, Simulations, and Science Learning in Formal Environments**
  Panel:
  Paul Horwitz, The Concord Consortium
  Nancy Songer, University of Michigan School of Education
  Rich Halverson, University of Wisconsin, Madison
  Committee discussion will follow.

5:15 p.m. **Closing Comments of Day 1**
  Margaret Honey, New York Hall of Science

5:30 p.m. **Adjourn**

October 7, 2009

8:30 a.m. **Discuss Agenda for the Day and Committee Comments**
  Margaret Honey, New York Hall of Science

9:00 a.m. **Learning Context: Gaming, Simulations, and Science Learning in Informal Environments**
  Author: Kurt Squire, University of Wisconsin, Madison
  Respondent Author: Mizuko Ito, University of California,
    Irvine
  Committee discussion will follow.

10:00 a.m. **Panel Discussion of Learning Context: Gaming, Simulations, and Science Learning in Informal Environments**
  Panel:
  Sasha Barab, Indiana University
  Reed Stevens, Northwestern University
  Daniel Edelson, National Geographic
  Committee discussion will follow.

11:00 a.m. Break

11:15 a.m. Assessment Issues for K-16 Science Learning in Simulations and Games: Measuring Performance Dynamically and Using Simulations/Games as Assessment Devices
>   **Authors:** Edys Quellmalz, Michael Timms, and Steven Schneider, WestEd
>   **Respondent Author:** John Behrens, Cisco Networking Academy

12:15 p.m. Participant Working Lunch
>   Margaret Honey, New York Hall of Science

Guiding Questions for Participants:
Respondents will consider these questions:

1. Where is there need for assessments, embedded in gaming and simulations, to guide and improve science learning?
2. Based on what has been discussed in all the previous sessions, are there additional sources of evidence the committee should be paying attention to? Are you aware of any citations or people whose work we should be paying attention to?
3. What ideas from yesterday and this morning have the most potential for science learning? Why?

Responses will be collected and given to a moderator, who will explain the major ideas from across the groups.

1:15 p.m. Panel Discussion: Opportunities for Needed Assessments with Gaming and Simulations for Science Learning in K-16 Education
>   **Panel:**
>   Ron Stevens, University of California, Los Angeles
>   Valerie Shute, Florida State University
>   Eva Baker, University of California, Los Angeles

2:15 p.m Moderator Report Out: Valuable Findings from Workshop Participants About Assessment with Gaming and Simulations for Science Learning and New Ideas (on yesterday's breakout questions)
>   **Moderator**: Jan Cannon-Bowers, University of Central Florida

2:30 p.m.   **Challenges of Bringing Gaming and Simulations to Scale for Science Learning**
        Author: Merrilea Mayo, Kauffman Foundation
        Respondent Author: Alan Gershenfeld, E-Line Ventures
        Respondent Author: Scot Osterweil, Massachusetts
            Institute of Technology
        Committee discussion will follow.

3:30 p.m.   **Break**

3:45 p.m.   **Panel Discussion: Challenges of Bringing Gaming and Simulations to Scale for Science Learning**
        Panel:
        Alex Chisolm, Learning Games Network
        Susan Zelman, Corporation for Public Broadcasting
        John Hight, Sony Computer Entertainment of America
        Committee discussion will follow.

4:45 p.m.   **Committee Report Out: Takeaways and Next Steps**

5:15 p.m.   **Final Closing Comments of the Workshop**
        Margaret Honey, New York Hall of Science

C

Biographical Sketches of Committee Members

Margaret A. Honey (*Chair*) is president and chief executive officer of the New York Hall of Science, a hands-on science and technology center. Her extensive work in the field of education technology includes serving as senior vice president for strategic initiatives and research at Wireless Generation, vice president of the Education Development Center, and director of its Center for Children and Technology. She codirected the Northeast and Islands Regional Education Laboratory, which helps educators, policy makers, and communities access and leverage the most current research about learning and K-12 education. She has directed numerous research projects, including efforts to identify teaching practices and assessments for 21st century skills; new approaches to teaching computational science in high schools; collaborations with the Public Broadcasting Service, the Corporation for Public Broadcasting, and some of the nation's largest public television stations; and investigations of data-driven decision-making tools and practices. With Bank Street College of Education faculty, she created one of the first Internet-based professional development programs. At the National Research Council, she chaired the Committee on IT Fluency and High School Graduation Outcomes: A Workshop. She has a B.A. in social theory from Hampshire College and M.A. and Ph.D. degrees in developmental psychology from Columbia University.

William B. Bonvillian is director of the Washington, DC, office of the Massachusetts Institute of Technology (MIT). He works to support the university's strong and historic relations with federal research and development (R&D) agencies and its role on national science policy. Prior to that position, he served for 17 years as a senior policy adviser in the U.S. Senate, working on science and technology policies and innovation issues. He worked extensively on legislation creating the U.S. Department of Homeland

Security, on intelligence reform, on defense and life science R&D, and on national competitiveness and innovation legislation. He has lectured and given speeches before numerous organizations on science, technology, and innovation questions, is on the adjunct faculty at Georgetown University, and has taught in this area at Georgetown, MIT, and George Washington University. He was the recipient of the IEEE Distinguished Public Service Award in 2007. At the National Research Council (NRC), he is a member of the Board on Science Education and served on the Committee on Modernizing the Infrastructure of the National Science Foundation's Federal Funds (R&D) Survey and the NRC's Exploring the Intersection of Science Education and the Development of 21st Century Skills. He has a B.A. in history from Columbia University, an M.A.R. in religion from Yale University, and a J.D. from the Columbia School of Law.

Janis Cannon-Bowers is associate professor of digital media at the University of Central Florida, a senior research scientist at its Institute for Simulation and Training, and founding director of its new Center for Research in Education, Art, Technology and Entertainment. She previously held the position of senior scientist for training systems for the U.S. Navy and has more than 17 years of experience conducting research on learning and performance in complex systems. She is an active researcher, with numerous scholarly publications and presentations, and serves on the editorial boards of several research journals. She is currently principal investigator on several efforts aimed at applying technology to K-12 education and workforce development, including grants from the National Science Foundation to investigate the development of synthetic learning environments and educational games for science education. She has a B.A. in psychology from Eckerd College and M.A. and Ph.D. degrees in industrial/organizational psychology from the University of South Florida.

Eric Klopfer is associate professor of science education at the Massachusetts Institute of Technology (MIT), and director of its Scheller Teacher Education Program, with a joint appointment at the MIT Media Lab. He is codirector of the MIT Education Arcade Initiative and the Scheller career development professor of science education and educational technology. His research focuses on the development and use of computer games and simulations for building understanding of science and complex systems. He created StarLogo TNG, a new platform for helping children create 3D simulations and games using a graphical programming language. On handheld computers, Klopfer's work includes participatory simulations, which embed users inside complex systems, and augmented reality simulations, which create a hybrid virtual/real space for exploring intricate scenarios in real time. He currently runs the StarLogo project, a desktop platform that enables students and teachers to create computer simulations of complex systems. He has a B.S. in biology from Cornell University and a Ph.D. in zoology from the University of Wisconsin, Madison.

James W. Pellegrino is liberal arts and sciences distinguished professor of cognitive psychology and distinguished professor of education at the University of Illinois, Chicago (UIC). He is codirector of UIC's Learning Sciences Research Institute. His current work is focused on analyses of complex learning and instructional environments, including those incorporating powerful information technology tools, with the goal of better understanding the nature of student learning and the conditions that enhance deep understanding. A special concern of his research is the incorporation of effective formative assessment practices, assisted by technology, to maximize student learning and understanding. At the National Research Council, Pellegrino has served on the Board on Testing and Assessment and cochaired the Committee on the Cognitive Science Foundations for Assessment, which issued the report *Knowing What Students Know: The Science and Design of Educational Assessment.* He recently helped The College Board build frameworks for curriculum, assessment, and professional development in advanced placement biology, chemistry, physics, and environmental science. He has a B.A. in psychology from Colgate University and M.A. and Ph.D. degrees from the University of Colorado.

Ray Perez oversees the Training & Education Technology Program and the Applied Instructional Research programs at the U.S. Office of Naval Research (ONR). At ONR, he manages a range of learning technology projects that include gaming, training, and simulations for military and educational purposes. The training projects are research based and include extensive use of computer technology, such as virtual reality, to provide realistic simulations and scenarios for U.S. naval forces. He has also been involved in the research, development, and implementation of specialized artificial intelligence techniques to emulate idealized instructors and tutors, or teammates and opponents. Some of his ONR work has involved collaborating with U.S. Department of Defense Education Activity schools. One recent program direction involves research on coaching strategies for fast-moving, dynamically evolving military tasks. He has a B.A. in psychology and M.A. and Ph.D. degrees in educational psychology from the University of California, Los Angeles.

Nichole Pinkard is visiting associate professor in the College of Computing and Digital Media at DePaul University. Previously, she was director of innovation for the University of Chicago's Urban Education Institute, where she played a leading role in creating optimal learning environments that span school, home, and community. She has led efforts to implement 1:1 computing in urban schools, to integrate new media into core instruction, and to create new media learning opportunities outside the school day. She is a recipient of the Jan Hawkins Award for Early Career Contributions to Humanistic Research and Scholarship in Learning Technologies and a National Science Foundation Early CAREER Fellowship. She serves on the Advisory Board of the Joan Ganz Cooney Center and on the National Advisory Committee for the Robert Wood Johnson Foundation's Health Games Research Program. Her current scholarly interests include the design and use of pedagogical-based social networks, new media literacy learning outcomes, and ecological models of learning. She has a B.S. in computer science from Stanford University and an M.S. in computer science and a Ph.D. in learning sciences from Northwestern University.

Daniel Schwartz is professor of education at Stanford University's School of Education. A member of the faculty there since 2000, he studies student understanding and representation and the ways that technology can facilitate learning. His work is at the intersection of cognitive science, computer science, and education, examining cognition and instruction in individual, cross-cultural, and technological settings. A theme throughout his research is how people's facility for spatial thinking can inform and influence processes of learning, instruction, assessment, and problem solving. He finds that new media make it possible to exploit spatial representations and activities in fundamentally new ways, offering an exciting complement to the verbal approaches that dominate educational research and practice. His current interest is in the creation and use of web-based tools for instruction. His current research focuses on mental models, instructional methods, transfer, child development, teachable agents, imagery and action, collaborative learning, and cognition. He has a teaching certificate from the University of California, Los Angeles, and a B.A. in philosophy and anthropology from Swarthmore College. He has an M.A. in computers and education and a Ph.D. in human cognition and learning from Columbia University.

Constance Steinkuehler is assistant professor in the Educational Communication and Technology Program of the curriculum and instruction department, School of Education, at the University of Wisconsin, Madison. Her research is on cognition, learning, and literacy in massively multiplayer online games. Current interests include "pop-cosmopolitanism" in online worlds and the intellectual practices that underwrite such a disposition, including informal scientific reasoning, collaborative problem solving, media literacy (as production, not just consumption), computational literacy, and the social learning mechanisms that support the development of such expertise (e.g., reciprocal apprenticeship, collective intelligence). She has B.A. degrees in mathematics, English, and religious studies from the University of Missouri, Columbia, and an M.A. in educational psychology and a Ph.D. in curriculum and instruction from the University of Wisconsin, Madision.

Carl E. Wieman (until March 2010) is distinguished professor of physics and winner of the 2001 Nobel Prize in physics for studies of the Bose-Einstein condensate. Currently he divides his time between the University of British Columbia, where he leads the Carl Wieman Science Education Initiative, and the University of Colorado, Boulder. The majority of his work is currently dedicated to reforming science teaching. He has been a member of the National Academy of Sciences since 1995. He is also a 2001 recipient of the National Science Foundation Director's Award for Distinguished Teaching Scholars as well as an award for distinguished teaching from the Carnegie Foundation. His research has involved the use of lasers and atoms to explore fundamental problems in physics. His physics research group at the University of Colorado, Boulder, has carried out a variety of precise laser spectroscopy measurements, including the most accurate measurements of parity nonconservation in atoms and the discovery of the anapole moment. He has also worked extensively on using laser light and magnetic fields to cool and trap atoms and investigating the physics of ultracold atoms. Since 2000, he has served on the National Task Force for Undergraduate Physics, which emphasizes improving undergraduate physics programs as a whole: introductory and advanced courses for all students, preparation of K-12 teachers, undergraduate research opportunities, and the recruitment and mentoring of students for diverse careers. At the National Research Council, he is the chair of the Board on Science Education and was a member of the study committee addressing the state of high school science laboratories. He has a Ph.D. from Stanford University.